D1600073

THE
RESCUE
OF THE
ROMANOVS

Books by Guy Richards

TWO RUBLES TO TIMES SQUARE (a novel)
IMPERIAL AGENT
THE HUNT FOR THE CZAR
THE RESCUE OF THE ROMANOVS

THE RESCUE OF THE ROMANOVS

Newly Discovered Documents
Reveal How Czar Nicholas II
and the
Russian Imperial Family
Escaped

BY GUY RICHARDS

THE DEVIN-ADAIR COMPANY
OLD GREENWICH, CONNECTICUT

DEDICATION

This book is dedicated to the more than 250 persons in six countries who helped to disinter this story from the mausoleums of times past. Their very existence, to say nothing of their readiness to work like mad for zero compensation, is cheerful assurance about the amount of energy available in the human family whenever a task in truth-seeking is under way. The energy seems to be especially responsive when the task threatens to demolish all the current axioms and theories about something, and that suggests that the race of man knows by instinct (a) that important truths are very hard to come by, and (b) that they are often hidden in colorful diversions and ingenious deceptions. Both these thoughts certainly apply here. To all these collaborators, I say thanks.

—G.R.

ISBN No. 0-8159-6717-9

Library of Congress Catalog Card Number: 74-27953

Manufactured in the United States of America

ANTICIPATING THE CRITICS: A STATEMENT BY THE PUBLISHER

Despite its immense number of new breakthroughs, this book is not offered as conclusive proof, at least in the legal sense of the word, that the last Imperial Family of Russia escaped the assassination so generally cited as their fate. It aspires, rather, to fill the void of evidence between two concepts hopelessly at variance with each other; one that the ex-Czar Nicholas II and six members of his family were shot by a Bolshevik firing squad on the night of July 16/17, 1918, at Ekaterinburg, Siberia; the other, that they were secretly rescued.

A substantial amount of circumstantial evidence supports each theory. The stalemate has been further solidified by the fact that seven governments, including those of the United States and Great Britain, disclaim any certain knowledge that the Romanovs were either murdered or saved.

Into the no man's land between the two theories, this book brings an overwhelming array of new evidence — some circumstantial, most of it hard core — favoring the rescue concept. In fact, it describes the rescue in the greatest detail. The new data are so massive in scope and specific in nature that if they don't clinch the case in the juridical sense, it is hard to imagine how they can fail to settle the issue in the mind of the general reader.

Why, then, is that not the same thing as deciding the issue in the full majesty and finality of the law?

Scholars will be quick to point out that some of the new evidence is unsubstantiated fifty-eight years after the Romanovs disappeared . . . that witnesses of the rescue have died . . . that no government will vouch for the accuracy of the Chivers messages which tell how the Imperial Family was spirited from its captors and smuggled out of Russia . . . that the original Lord Hardinge letter which traces the escape route for King George V in June 1919 has not been turned over to experts outside of government circles for validation of its Foreign Office seal, its Hardinge signature, its paper, typewriter or typeface.

But the same objections apply even more to the evidence backing the assassination theory. No bodies, skulls, teeth or identifiable bones of the Romanovs ever were found. The late Francis Camps, whom the British Broadcasting Corporation termed in its 1972 TV documentary on the Romanovs "the most distinguished forensic expert in Britain," riddled the "facts" given in support of the murder as totally unworthy of belief. He said that they wouldn't stand the chance of acceptance in any British court and he labeled the reasoning followed by the chief of the official Russian investigation of the case as "rubbish" and an example of the practice of "the gentle art of self-deception to an incredible degree." Even so, the weight of the years and the seeming nonappearance of the survivors long have biased world opinion towards the assassination theory.

Only a small fraction of the new material in this book is likely to incite the skepticism of scholars. The rest derives from sources that are as fresh to the case as they are easy to verify.

For example, the Naval Intelligence Command (formerly the Office of Naval Intelligence) never has released the stories of its agents by name and mission and has no intention of doing so. It claims that there is too much sensitive matter involved. (ONI men often worked for the State Department as special agents. Some later joined the CIA.) It was a monumental sleuthing job to get the facts about the American Naval Intelligence agents in Revolutionary Russia which are presented here for the first time. To obtain them the author had to ransack the files and the memories of men in a half dozen Federal agencies, and it took him more than ten months to track down from one old address to another the descendants of just one of the men — the late Commander Sergius M. Riis. But the results were well worth the time.

Skeptical objectors will have a most uncomfortable experience trying to dismiss the testimony of Hubert M. Limbrick, former captain's messenger on H.M.S. *Calypso*. Over and over again he picked out the features of the Czar's daughter, Anastasia, from old group photographs of the Romanovs as being those of the young woman whom his ship carried in the captain's cabin, guarded day and night by Cossacks, from Odessa to Venice in 1919. A former City Councilman of Thunder Bay, Ontario, Limbrick is still very much alive.

Objectors will have a similar hard time of it trying to explain away some documents recently translated from the Russian after being presented by Bayard Kilgour to the Houghton Library at Harvard. The translator was a representative of the *Sunday Times* of London. He discovered that the documents were interviews with various members of the Imperial Family in the weeks after their "assassination" and that they had been reported to the staff of the official investigator of the "murder" — Judge Nicholas A. Sokolov — but for some reason had been omitted from his book.

Doubters likewise won't find it easy to lay to rest the ghost of Roy C. Woods of Scottsdale, Arizona. He, too, is still alive at the age of 95. He states that he was on a special mission for Secretary of State Charles Evans Hughes when he went to Poland in 1923. There novelist Kenneth Roberts met Woods, and later recounted in his memoirs the story of Mr. Woods' negotiations with another daughter of the Czar, Tatiana, on plans to bring her and a collection of art treasures to the United States at a point in time approximately five years after her reported murder. The plans fell through.

Nor will the skeptics find it simple to cope with the blunt truths relayed by an agent of the French Deuxième Bureau who passed back to his headquarters in Paris the essence of interviews with Nicholas and Alexandra long after their official entombment. Nor will they be heartened to discover that a fortnight before the Romanovs' "assassination" the German Kaiser, Wilhelm II, ordered his agents in Russia, including his man in Kiev, Count Alvensleben, to be forewarned of a staged execution of Nicholas "between the 16th and 20th of July" which was designed for the ex-Czar's own safety, and which they were to understand to be false but were to speak and behave publicly as if it were genuine.

The list of other such items bearing on the rescue is far too long to be encapsulated here. It is up to the reader to proceed through instance after instance until he will most surely pass that point of no return beyond which the murder of the Romanovs is no longer a credible story, legal or not. The truth is that the heart of the law is the jury system and both the jury and the judge can only rule on evidence that has been submitted to them. Most of the evidence in this book has never before been submitted to more than a few persons. Much of it is new to all but a few insiders.

Mr. Richards — a veteran journalist — believes his role is to correct that situation with a vengeance. He has done so in a relentlessly low-key manner which permits the reader to reach his own conclusions without being coerced. The assortment of characters one meets in the process are worth the price of admission by themselves — those two puzzled but enthusiastic old friends from the House of Commons, Peter Bessell and Jeremy Thorpe . . . the three old Naval Intelligence cronies, one of whom arrived for his plebe year at Annapolis with a horse and a valet and another of whom ran away to sea at the age of twelve and got such a good schooling in old St. Petersburg that for years he spoke Russian better than his native American. . . . Major William Peer-Groves, British agent, orientalist and R.A.F. pilot, who loved to wear a kimono when he wasn't making an official call on the ex-Czar's mother, the Dowager Empress Marie, and signing her visitors' register at Malta's San Antonio Palace (Peer-Groves' daughter, by the way, is alive and well in England and recalls what her father said about the rescue of the Romanovs). The Dowager Empress Marie, herself, is someone to cause doubters distress. Not only did she go to her death telling close friends that her son and his family had never been executed, but in 1919 she told her British aide in Malta, Lt. Robert Ingham, that she knew exactly where her son was hiding.

In another sense the book is a do-it-yourself detective story. It employs patience and shoe leather in making the rounds. In these days, when government bureaucracies are from five to ten times bigger and more abundant than the 1918 variety, one winces in grim sympathy as Richards and his research associates wade through the mire of the British checkpoints: the Admiralty, the Board of Trade, the Royal Air Force, the Foreign Office, Public Record Office, House of Commons — and then tackle the ramparts of the old Anglo-American Alliance in Washington where the agencies are even bigger and more numerous: the Navy, Marine Corps, ONI, the Naval War College, State Department, Foreign Service, Defense Department, CIA, Justice Department, National Archives, Library of Congress, Senate, Veterans Administration, National Personnel Records Center, etc.

Nearly three generations after the event, what imaginable gains — the reader asks himself — could come from such far-ranging rambles around the briar patches?

As a minimum, there emerged at least three discoveries that were bridges to many more:

Through a friend in the British Foreign Office, Peter Bessell made the discovery that there was a secret codicil in the Brest-Litovsk Treaty of peace between the Germans and the Bolsheviks in March, 1918 by which the latter agreed to the Kaiser's demands that the Imperial Family of Russia (his relatives) be granted safe passage out of the country. That, of course, gives sound reason as to why Lenin's agents would lend their support to Allied agents in redeeming the terms of the codicil. Failure to do so would have required the Bolsheviks to face the resumption of the rapid German military advance. The Bolshevik leaders could have been wiped out. (Our State Department says that it was never let in on this codicil in the

Russo-German treaty. President Wilson undoubtedly was, however. As for the British, their Secret Service in those days often delivered items like this before the Foreign Office even knew of their existence. That could account for Whitehall having a copy of the codicil while Foggy Bottom is still searching for it. But it's a fair bet that the CIA *does* have it by now.)

Through an ex-Foreign Service source, Richards learned why for years State Department spokesmen have been telling members of Congress and reporters from the media that all State's files from the World War I era have been declassified and placed in the National Archives. This is simply not true. All of State's *sensitive* files from the World War I period, and particularly those about its special agents, were transferred to the CIA after its formation in 1947. Along with them went Robert Bannerman, former Chief Special Agent of State.

There they are to this day, with a few exceptions. The CIA was obliging enough to confirm the fact to Richards. Either State's spokesmen didn't know this or were hanging on the technicality that the documents are now the CIA's, not State's.

With assistance from the CIA, and from the Manhattan chapter of the American Red Cross, it was possible to use a very stale address in Brooklyn as the starting point of a nationwide hunt for the widow and son of one of the American agents, Commander Sergius M. Riis. The search was hampered in its early stages by finding that his widow had followed her husband to the grave. Just short of a year after it started, the hunt ended in Plantation, Florida, a suburb of Fort Lauderdale. Commander Riis's only child, Earl, was located there. He flew to New York and read the fifty-six-year-old Chivers messages from start to finish. He was visibly moved. In them, he said, he spotted numerous phrases and expressions which his father frequently used in his rather unique style of English (the elder Riis was schooled in Russia).

"There's no question that my father was there at the time," said Earl. "I have no doubt but that he could have written those long dispatches."

This was a thrilling wind-up for the author's ten-year-long peregrination in search of the facts — the son reading what he gathered was his father's account of the rescue of the Romanovs.

But probably just as dramatic to the reader will be the author's achievements in restructuring from the new facts he had to go on the tactics and motivations of the grand strategy used in one of history's most smoothly-meshed disappearing acts — and how those tactics dovetail with what had already surfaced.

To all of this, including the existence of the Chivers messages, Henry Kissinger pleads ignorance. In the scenario spelled out in the following pages the reader can reach his own opinion on the real extent of that ignorance. The Secretary of State, for example, knows Senator Claiborne Pell quite well. The Senator is a member of the Foreign Relations Committee. I think it is significant that Dr. Kissinger decided to turn over the task of answering the Senator's inquiry regarding the Chivers Papers and his stepfather's possible participation in the Romanovs' rescue to an underling, Linwood Holton. Perhaps Kissinger was trying to save himself later embarrassment. From reading Mr. Holton's response one gets the impression that Mr. Holton's ignorance of the subject is as real as it is all-embracing. He doesn't even refer to the considerable scholarship by four different authors who concluded that the Romanovs must have escaped.

By continuing to refuse to admit truths which are scrawled all over the roof, aren't the sovereign nations involved making themselves look more and more ridiculous, thereby adding new justification to the scorn in which many of their statesmen are held nowadays? After all, a matter for which there were good reasons for secrecy in 1918 can become a matter whose continued secrecy in the 1970s is nothing less than a scandal. For it is only natural for suspicions to be aroused that private interests with a great deal to hide have managed to prevail over the Government. In default of all other explanations, that seems to be the story here.

The moment is timely for delving into the Romanov Case. In the national capital the issue of information withheld from Congress and the people has become a fiery one, second in interest only to ways of solving economic troubles.

In short, the case could prove to be a textbook classic for Congressional study as one impregnated with traces of many, many others that cover a much shorter time span. There are many reasons why the Romanov Case is more significant now than it was in 1918 and 1919, but none is more so than the questions of who sat on the synthetic coffins of the Romanovs every time someone tried to lift the lids, why it was done, and where the orders came from.

Old Greenwich, Conn. —DEVIN A. GARRITY

CONTENTS

PREFACE

According to a series of coded messages held for years in a White House safe, neither Bolshevik gunmen nor any other executioners ended the lives of ex-Czar Nicholas II, his wife Alexandra and their five children. Their widely-publicized "massacre" on the night of July 16/17, 1918, now can be unmasked as one of history's greatest hoaxes.

According to the Chivers Papers — the code name of the messages — none of the Imperial Family was murdered in that bullet-riddled basement room of Ipatiev House at Ekaterinburg, Siberia, where the walls and floors reportedly were splattered with blood. The picture of the room has become a textbook stereotype of the tragic end of a dynasty. These more than one hundred highly descriptive pages, most of them from an American agent on the scene, contradict historians on almost all vital points.

They record how Lenin's deputies collaborated with operatives of the Japanese, Americans, White Russians and Cossacks to deliver the Romanovs to a British ship at the Black Sea port of Odessa on February 16, 1919. That is precisely seven months to the day after they disappeared from Ekaterinburg.

The identity of the American agent is withheld. His reports include a graphic and diary-like chronicle of a staggering secret journey by car and truck which covered 1,800 miles of rugged Russian countryside. It began in Siberia's snowclad Ural Mountains six days before Christmas, 1918. It ended in the much milder seaside climate of Odessa on February 14, 1919.

To facilitate the escape from Ipatiev House, the lives of two members of the Romanovs' personal retinue were sacrificed. Their names are not given, but they were shot after the Imperial Family left, and their flesh and blood undoubtedly provided some of the stage effects of the alleged massacre. (Four members of the Imperial Family's old entourage were with them on July 16: Dr. Eugene Botkin, the physician; Anna Demidova, a maidservant, and Trupp and Kharitonov, two manservants.) At Odessa, the pilgrims from a lost empire stayed in a private residence commandeered for U.S. officials in the area, which was then controlled by the French Army. Two days later the British Navy took the Romanovs away.

They vanish from the scope of the Chivers Papers on the night of February 16, 1919. They promptly appear on the screen on a letter signed by a British diplomat. This British version — a June, 1919 letter from Lord Hardinge to King George V — picks them up at Odessa. It drops off three of the seven members of the family along the way, but doesn't state where. It takes Nicholas and his daughters Olga, Tatiana and Marie on a meandering trip through Constantinople, Sofia, Vienna and Linz, Austria, and leaves them at Breslau (then Germany, now Poland) on May 10, 1919.

What became of Alexandra, Alexei and Anastasia? Where were they left off? It could have been a number of places, but a good surmise is somewhere in Bulgaria, the nation which had made great progress since it had cut loose from the Ottoman Empire, but had bet wrong in World War I and allied itself with Germany. The Bulgarian monarch at the time of the Romanovs' arrival was King Boris III, a youngster in his middle twenties who was a godson of the former Czar of all the Russias.

All told, with eight American guards joining the party, and with the Japanese continuing to provide security with the help of the Russian Reds, Whites and loyalist Cossacks, this heretofore unpublicized journey out of wintry Siberia must comprise one of the strangest treks in the history of royalty.

The public has been denied the truth about the sunset of the Romanovs for more than half a century. Now, through the Chivers Papers, it gets the story from a participant in the spectacular rescue — the U.S. agent — whose skill in reportage is more than a match for his momentous tale.

He doesn't seem to miss a trick. Roadway mishaps, bouts of illness (Alexandra, the former Czarina, among others, got the flu), a scary stopover in an abandoned army camp, conversational sallies with Nicholas or one of his daughters, and the joy of luxuriating at Tambov in the Black Earth belt, where they found their first beds and the comforts of home, are all described.

Although the agent was filing his reports to be wirelessed in code to Secretary of State Robert Lansing for the information of President Wilson, apparently he felt not the least inhibited about including all the spicier items of family chitchat. His words illuminate poignancy, human frailty and personal humiliation. In one message the ex-Czarina is found in an imperious rage over being jounced along the terrible roads on a springless seat like a farmer's daughter in a haycart. For example:

July 18, 1918

"His M. (Nicholas II) will not be known without his whiskers and with his hair so long . . . The G.D.s (four daughters of Nicholas and Alexandra) were most compliant and snipped off each other's hair. The Grand D. (Czarevich Alexei) has no disguise and we fear he must be detected."

September 14, 1918

"Daily it is more difficult to be sure these wireless codes are sent to you. . . . The Grand D. was not so ill but is listless and still stops in bed all day. He is of moody disposition and demands at all times to be treated as a prince when he is then more friendly."

December 18, 1918

"Tomorrow we take leave of this house and place and start upon the journey to the southern shore. . . . It is now below freezing temperature outside and snow cover roads and trees alike. . . . When you next may hear is now in the hands of God."

December 30, 1918

"Arrived Kungar. Journey bad. Snow and slipping on ice. . . . Food bad, provided by field kitchens as agreed."

February 17, 1919

"And now it is time for me to write a last dispatch in triumph. All, as you know, has gone well to plan. The journey [is] over and if the risks were big the consequence [is] more than rewarding."

The American agent passes along Nicholas's views about the German and Bolshevik leaders. He recounts his own admiration for the courageous conduct of Nicholas's daughter Marie. He even gets as agitated as any other American tourist far from home when the group runs out of money. Urgently he asks for more and gets $150,000, half from the Japanese and half from the U.S. The British were asked to chip in a few more pounds, too, but they declined. They would pick up the tab, they said, from the Black Sea onward. All this simply could not have been taking place if we are to believe the historians. On the say-so of textbooks and military studies of World War I, by the winter of 1918-19 the seven Romanovs were long since dead and their flesh had been consumed by the Siberian earth.

The commonly-accepted report has them routed out of bed around midnight by Jacob Yurovsky, leader of the Cheka Guard at Ipatiev House, and led to a basement room. There they were killed by the gunfire of a special squad of "Letts," of whom at least five were Magyars recruited from Austro-Hungarian army war prisoners. On July 20 the Bolshevik leaders in Moscow made an official announcement that Nicholas had been executed. A year later they stated that the whole family had been killed.

Though no Romanov bodies ever were found, some of the Imperial Family's personal possessions were discovered in the shaft of the abandoned "Four Brothers Mine" about fourteen miles from Ekaterinburg. Among the articles exhumed from the mine were belt buckles believed to be those of Nicholas and his son; a lens from Alexandra's spectacles; scorched parts of corsets; a jeweled cross, a platinum earring, pearls and fragments of emeralds and sapphires which may have belonged to Alexandra or her daughters. Only one "corpse" was identified — that of the Family's pet spaniel dog.

This book is primarily the record of how acutely difficult it was for the agents of several countries to rescue one ex-czar when the tide turned against him. Officials of monarchies and republics alike felt they would be frightfully embarrassed if their solicitude towards Nicholas in 1918 and 1919 ever became known. Thus this is also a chronicle of the wily dissimulation, the creative deceit and the devious suppressive measures used, not only in the rescue itself, but in official efforts exerted over more than fifty-seven years to sustain the pretense that it never happened. The dead weight and magnetic appeal of Romanov funds in various banks here and abroad has figured in the political suppression.

The Rescue of the Romanovs is being published at a time when both Americans and Britons have found new reasons to bemoan the acts of their governments, many of them illegal, which have been kept hidden through claims that "national security" was involved. It is no accident that it required the labors of more than 250 persons in six countries, over a ten-year period, to exhume the truth about the Romanovs. Not the least of these were two members of the House of Commons, Peter Bessell and Jeremy Thorpe, both members of the Liberal Party.

The rescue of the Imperial Family was a venture to which the United States made lavish contributions in manpower, money and diplomatic pressure, but to now has maintained secrecy about. Let the reader decide for himself whether the government of a nation that claims to be an open society should have the right to withhold the truth for so many years and thus perpetuate a giant fraud on its citizens and on history.

PART I

THE HUNTERS

CHAPTER 1

PETER BESSELL

It was 1964 when I first became interested in the fate of the last Imperial Family of Russia. That was because of an exceptionally interesting espionage case involving Lieutenant Colonel Michal Goleniewski, a defector from Polish Military Intelligence. He claimed that neither Czar Nicholas II nor any member of his family was assassinated in 1918, as the Bolsheviks announced. Quite blandly, without batting his hazel eyes or tweaking his guardsman moustache, he said that he was the long-missing Czarevich Alexei. (More probably he is a relative.)

Since his record as a secret agent was solidly documented, I tried to keep a straight face about the Czarevich part. I wrote a book on his case, *Imperial Agent*, which gave the reader material for a number of options in deciding who Goleniewski really was.

I became more interested in the fate of the Romanovs after *Imperial Agent* brought in a surprising amount of new circumstantial evidence indicating that their widely-publicized "murder" was a hoax, and I wrote another book, *The Hunt for the Czar*, which featured this new material from all over the world. Its publication moved everything about the case from low gear to high.

I became absolutely fascinated with the subject of the Romanovs when this second book led, of all places, to a member of the British House of Commons who held out hope of obtaining official documents on the secret rescue of the Romanovs by a team of foreign agents.

Thereupon the search for the facts was transformed from the plodding routines of a writer-researcher into a four-year-long detective story that spanned the Atlantic, embraced the chancelleries of seven nations, involved such unlikely fellow-hunters as representatives of the French Deuxième Bureau; the then opposition hero, Jeremy Thorpe, leader of Britain's Liberal Party; Tony Summers and Tom Mangold of the British Broadcasting Corporation; Secretary of State Henry A. Kissinger; Senator Claiborne Pell, a liberal Democrat from Rhode Island; Congressman John M. Ashbrook of Ohio, a right-wing Republican; the State Department; the CIA; the White House, and the foreign ministries of the Soviet Union, Sweden, France, Japan, Britain and West Germany.

No debonair writer of fiction would make the mistake of trying to crowd so many sovereign states and divergent personalities into one narrative. So I owe everyone an apology; though I am not debonair and haven't written any murder mysteries, the worldwide escalation was not my own doing. The story did it to itself. I can state honestly that of all the assignments I had as a newspaperman, none compared with the Romanov Case for bringing so many repercussions so quickly, and over so many square miles of the earth's surface, after a modest beginning in New York.

The four-year-long detective story started with a telephone call to my Manhattan apartment in April, 1970. The date was only a few weeks after my second book had reached the stores. In an upper-class British accent, the voice declared itself to be that of Peter Bessell, member of the House of Commons from Cornwall.

Mr. Bessell said he was an amateur historian who had spent a lot of time on the Habsburgs. He added that he had just finished reading my book with much interest and felt that I should have made the fifteenth chapter — the one about Judge Nicholas A. Sokolov's probe of the "assassination" at Ekaterinburg — the first chapter. If I had done so, he ventured, he would have developed the feeling much sooner that something should be done in Parliament to smoke out the truth from the British government.

Mr. Bessell's voice intrigued me. It was a voice to conjure with. Though it was cultivated, it was free of that clipped, adenoidal tone of overculture that one associates with Oxford dons and Anglican bishops. It was much closer to the more coherent theatre-English of Sir Laurence Olivier. It also had something else going for it. It was the voice of the first member of the House of Commons who had ever shown enough interest in my work to track me down and say so. I was flattered.

I told Mr. Bessell that I was delighted at the thought of smoking out the British Government. Since my book was about to be published in England, unless the Government invoked the Official Secrets Act to ban it, I replied that I would be most grateful if a member of the House of Commons could be counted on my side.

Mr. Bessell said he was in New York on business. I invited him for lunch and we settled on an early date. Before we met I consulted the British *Who's Who* and found a generous stretch of type about "Peter Joseph Bessell, born 24th Aug. 1921 . . . property financial broker" with offices at 41 Pall Mall and a home in Cornwall.

There were other pertinent notations: Mr. Bessell was married and had two children . . . he headed Peter Bessell Ltd., a financial brokerage concern, and was director of several other companies . . . a member of the Liberal Party, he had been first elected to the House of Commons in 1964 from the Bodmin district of Cornwall . . . he had been a member of a number of Select Committees of Parliament . . . in World War II he had been a lecturer for the Ministry of Information to His Majesty's armed forces from 1943 to 1945.

That last item was revealing. Conforming with my impression that his voice and political career suggested a polished speaker and debater, it showed that back in those bleak days of World War II, when His Majesty's Government was trying to determine the best use for the young Cornishman's talents, it decided against combat at sea or ashore in favor of his vocal prowess.

He was precisely punctual for the luncheon engagement. I found him to be a short, good-looking, high-strung individual with the bedside manner and aggressive posture so beloved by shy and passive women. Twenty years ago Frank Sinatra was just such a man. In short, Mr. Bessell was charming. It took him no more than a few sallies of conversation to get across the idea — but without unseemly braggadocio — that he was well connected in London and Washington. He casually mentioned that he had met and discoursed with Presidents Johnson and Nixon. He said he even had a passably pleasant acquaintance with Henry Kissinger ever since the two had met in Washington while Bessell was a member of a committee on East-West trade.

He seemed just what the doctor ordered for opening doors in high places everywhere. When we parted he said he would give a high priority to the Romanov matter and would try to get some questions about it tabled in the House of Commons after he returned shortly to London.

As far as I know he was as good as his word. I soon received from him an airmail letter from London on House of Commons stationery, containing four questions about the Romanovs. The most significant was this one:

"Mr. Peter Bessell (Bodmin) asks the Prime Minister whether Her Majesty's Government has any evidence to suggest that the former Czar Nicholas II or any of the members of the former Russian Imperial Family, who were presumed to have been killed at Ekaterinburg in the Soviet Union in 1918, have survived and if so, will he circulate in the Official Report details of such evidence."

The other three questions were about Michal Goleniewski, the Romanov claimant, and whether or not the Chancellor of the Exchequer held monies from Nicholas II in the "Accounts of the Bank of England."

According to Mr. Bessell, the Clerk in the House of Commons deemed the questions unacceptable in the form presented. He suggested a number of rewordings. Time was consumed in this process of dickering — so much time, in fact, that Parliament was dissolved on May 29, 1970 for a new election in which Mr. Bessell had already announced his intention not to succeed himself.

But he made a number of other moves on the Romanov Case. Through personal contacts in the government, he was able to determine that there was a secret codicil in the Treaty of Brest-Litovsk (signed March 3, 1918) in which the Bolsheviks agreed to the German demand that "safe passage" be granted "to the Imperial Family of Russia."

Separated as he was from Parliament after Prime Minister Heath's Government took over on July 2, 1970, Mr. Bessell continued to give a great deal of attention to the Romanovs during that summer and fall. On a visit to Malta he interviewed the long-retired Army Captain Robert Ingham. He is the officer who, as a young lieutenant in 1919, heard Nicholas's mother, the Dowager Empress Marie, state positively that she knew her son and his family were safe. Mr. Bessell, a signatory to the British Official Secrets Act, came away from Malta quite positive that Captain Ingham, also a signatory to the Official Secrets Act, knew that the Romanovs had been rescued and precisely how.

Back in London Mr. Bessell's interest in the case became noised around Fleet Street, and this led to the publication of several interviews with him on the subject. These, in turn, inspired wider coverage by reporters assigned to do their own investigations, resulting in a new spate of articles and an especially comprehensive study which became seven pages, including the page one lead, of the March 7, 1971 Sunday magazine section of *The Observer*. With the appearance of *Hunt for the Czar* in England from the presses of Peter Davies, Ltd., another series of articles appeared in the media and there began a steady stream of correspondence about the Romanovs in the personal columns of the newspapers with the largest volume in the *London Times*. Off and on it lasted nearly three months.

When some of these letters reported that relics and possibly a bone or two of the Romanovs were buried in certain foreign cemeteries, Mr. Bessell arranged for another interested person, British novelist Susanna Hoe, to investigate the cemeteries named. She covered all of them — in France, Belgium and the United Kingdom. Her report, which was published in the *London Times*, among other media, was totally negative.

Mr. Bessell's greatest achievement in London was to get the British Broadcasting Corporation rolling. A research team from BBC sought him out. When the BBC men were through interviewing him, they started on a reportorial safari, complete with producer Tony Summers, reporter-narrator Tom Mangold and a camera crew that ranged over Europe, Canada and the United States and resulted in an hour-long telecast, "The File on the Tsar." It made its debut in the United Kingdom on January 23, 1972. On the morning of its showing, the London *Sunday Times* came out with a two-page spread asserting that papers now in the Houghton Library at Harvard University proved that Judge Nicholas Sokolov had omitted from his report on the "assassination" a number of interviews with persons who had seen one or more of the Imperial Family alive in different places long after July 17, 1918.

The telecast was tailored right down the middle of the case. Tom Mangold was the narrator, and he presented what he thought was all the important evidence pro and con the assassination. Most of the pro material was familiar. It boiled down to the question, "Well, if they survived, where are they?" It offered the findings of the Sokolov Report, but it submitted to the viewer several experts who ridiculed Sokolov's summations. Most notable of these was the late Professor Francis Camps of Scotland Yard. He was introduced as "the most distinguished forensic specialist in Britain."

Point by point he annihilated Sokolov's claims that a group of men could remove all traces of the bodies of eleven persons, including bones, skulls and dentures, with the help of petrol and sulphuric acid. He observed that "I utterly reject" the account which he described as a "classic example of a report wholly prejudiced and in favor of a set of required conclusions. These conclusions, based as they are on a series of assumptions, are inaccurate."

Professor Camps died a few months after giving this testimony.

The BBC telecast broke new ground on the anti-assassination side of the story. Profiting from his interviews with French government officials on the case, Mr. Mangold submitted a report from an agent of the Deuxième Bureau describing the scene in a hiding place seventeen months after their "assassination" in which Nicholas is found to be in fine health, indeed "strongwilled and very determined," but Alexandra "in a state of total collapse."

The BBC production rendered another service in the overall, modern detective story. It reminded viewers that the Czar's valet, who died three months after the imperial fadeout at Ekaterinburg, told several persons that he *knew* servants alone had been murdered in the cellar as a cover for the rescue of Nicholas and his family. This took on heightened importance in the United States, a few months later, when the Chivers Papers were first seen by Mr. Bessell, according to his reports to me. They, too, conveyed the same news: namely, that two members of the Romanov entourage were killed and their flesh and blood presumably used to provide the stage effects of a family massacre.

The name of the valet was Terenti Ivanovich Chemodurov. The best reference to him on this point can be found in the Sokolov Report and in Count Paul Benckendorff's book *Last Days at Tsarskoe Selo*.

In its telecast, the BBC gave the formal replies of seven nations to its questions about whether their governments knew if the Romanovs were assassinated or not. Every one ducked; none came up with a yea or nay response. They were the United States, the United Kingdom, the Soviet Union, France, West Germany, Japan and Sweden. The American reply was about the same as all the others: "The Department of State has not formulated an official position as to whether the Tsar was, in fact, killed in Ekaterinburg."

The Soviet Foreign Ministry simply referred its British questioners to the notes on the subject in the Soviet Historical Encyclopedia, which states: "The Ekaterinburg Council took a decision to execute Tsar Nicholas, his family and retinue." The Foreign Ministry spokesman declined to expand on whether or not the council's decision was carried out.

Among the noble personages who graced the BBC show were the Grand Duke Vladimir of Russia, a resident of Spain who claims to be the legal heir of the Czar's throne; and Lord Louis Mountbatten who, as the nephew of Czarina Alexandra, used to call the Czar "Uncle Nicky."

They voiced gentle disagreement with the oft-expressed conviction of Nicholas's mother, the Dowager Empress Marie, that her son and family "are alive" and that she knew where they were being hidden. But both Vladimir and Lord Louis quickly demurred when asked directly by Tom Mangold if they thought the eighty-one-year-old lady had become demented before she died in October, 1928 at the Danish palace of Hvidore.

"No, no," Vladimir responded, "I don't think she was unbalanced at all." Lord Louis agreed.

By the time the BBC telecast had been shown (and it later appeared in other parts of the world as far away as Australia), Peter Bessell had been widely identified in England as a man responsible for much of the new ruckus over the Romanovs. It was quite right that he should be. In my files I have a cablegram from him shortly after he made his first contact with the BBC. It reads:

URGENT PLEASE AIRMAIL IMPERIAL AGENT TO TONY SUMMERS TELE-
CASTS LONDON PS4 FILM PRODUCTION 24 HOURS LIME GROVE STOP BBC
MOUNTING MAJOR NATIONWIDE HUNT PROGRAMME FOR END JULY
LETTER FOLLOWS   PETER

In fact, he was so widely branded as the chief revivalist that it worried him. At least one bank in Paris, London and New York reportedly holds undistributed funds in the account of Czar Nicholas II. Conceivably they might not take kindly to the surfacing of the "no-assassination" facts.

"My wife, Pauline, has warned me several times," he told me on one of his frequent trips to New York in 1972, "that I could get chewed up for rocking a boat that's so close to the Royal Family."

"Who could chew you up?" I asked.

"Oh, the financial community. It doesn't like to see any of its members get into public controversies like this — things that are off the beaten path of our responsibilities."

He explained that his business made him a middleman between British banks that supplied capital for investments in the United Kingdom and elsewhere. He was in the process of opening a new suite of offices at 685 Fifth Avenue, New York. It would not be unreasonable to suppose, he said, that some weighty personage in London could drop a hint to some of the banks to drag out all negotiations with his company and, for a while, ultimately decline to underwrite any of his clients' projects.

This was about the time that a new horizon opened up — the chance of obtaining United States documents on the Romanov Case. I mention it now only because it relates to a later mystery inside the whole Romanov conundrum — Peter Bessell's disappearance, in 1974, from all his old haunts in Britain and America.

Sooner or later, I knew from experience, a matter like this is apt to veer into the realm of documents — real or forged — and for some time there had lurked in the back of my mind the notion that Bessell could be a British agent. Knowing how the British Secret Service had operated in Russia in the World War I period, implanting a man in every conceivable facet of the Revolution, and having read Richard Deacon's *A History of the British Secret Service*, I was alerted to the possibility that MI-6 might follow its classic pattern for dealing with the Americans who were coming a little too close to something it wanted kept under wraps.

This pattern, I reasoned, could be as follows:

Send a man over to join the American team. Have him give the Americans praise, moral support and some help. Have him promise them a lot more . . . drop lavish hints about access to high government officials . . . dangle in front of them official documents that might be produced. Then when they reach for the bait, unload on them a batch of phony but official-looking papers which they will publicize as genuine. When the papers are exposed as blatant fakes, the Americans will be revealed as gullible fools. Their whole effort will be pictured as a quixotic fiasco worthy only of laughter and scorn — and it will be another half century before anyone will dare advance the theory again that the Romanovs survived Ekaterinburg.

In revolutionary Russia, for one example, the British had suckered the Americans into buying the "Sisson Papers" from Commander Ernest Boyce, a British secret agent. These papers were widely publicized in the United States. They were — along with nonfakes — designed to prove that the Bolsheviks, after gaining power, remained faithful stewards of the German General Staff. (See *Ace of Spies* by R. B. Lockhart.)

The truth was that by early 1972 Peter Bessell had qualified himself in all the opening rounds of the MI-6 formula. In the first place, he was a platinum-plated, smooth actor. He behaved like a British agent. He had joined the American team with polite enthusiasm. He had stirred up such a storm of publicity in Britain for what had started as an American enterprise that he had even decided to backtrack a little by rejecting the BBC's invitation to appear in its telecast.

But if Bessell was a British agent, I asked myself, wasn't there a chance that he had already overdone his role? As an MI-6 operative, his assignment would be to demolish the Americans but leave himself unscathed. This program, then, was not proceeding along classic lines. Mr. Bessell's broad, public identification with the case in Britain thenceforward meant that he could not lead the Americans to disaster without bringing it on himself, too, and wrecking his business along with it.

No, I thought, MI-6 men — for all their variable bits of derring-do — are not encouraged to court suicide.

There was another aspect which seemed to provide its own safeguards when Mr. Bessell first brought word of U.S. documents on the case. These documents, he said, were going to be declassified by the White House and released to the public. Papers that are turned over to the National Archives in this manner are not necessarily guaranteed to tell wholly truthful stories. Indeed, disclaimers of this responsibility for accuracy of the contents are generally stamped on the documents by the archivists. But the mere act of official declassification authenticates them as genuine government papers which are ready for evaluation by scholars and historians. This is a solid insurance against forgeries, counterfeits and palpable frauds.

In those early days of 1972, after the BBC's telecast, the main thrust of the investigation shifted back to the western side of the Atlantic, and so did Peter Bessell. He opened an office on Fifth Avenue, left his London office in the hands of aides and moved his own residence to New York. At this stage of developments our relationship had grown much closer.

I had become very fond of the handsome little Briton with the William Gladstone voice. He was as arrogant as a young general on his first campaign, but witty, idealistic, enormously well-read and highly stimulating. His impatience with secretaries and petty functionaries would often fire him into girlish rages which were, strangely enough, as amusing to the targets as they were to spectators, not only because of their eloquence, but because they seemed to be bereft of malice. My wife and I invested what was, for us, a generous sum in his newly-formed American company, Peter Bessell, Inc. He asked me if I would help to sponsor his application for U.S. citizenship, and I agreed.

Somewhere along in here, Mr. Bessell let it be known that he had rendered a substantial service to the U.S. Government a year or two before, involving some foreign transactions and high finance. He said he had been drawing on that old favor, highly regarded in the White House, when he asked Henry Kissinger if he would launch a search for any Romanov papers in the various agencies of the executive branch. That was in late 1970 or early 1971, and long before Mr. Kissinger had become Secretary of State. But it was in 1972 that the request — on Mr. Bessell's say-so — began to bear fruit. Each of his reports to me about it was generally made after a trip to the national capital by the jaunty Cornishman. Sometimes, however, he said he conferred with his contact at the White House over the bugproofed telephone at the U.S. Mission to the United Nations on First Avenue. I went there with him on one occasion.

On one or two of his trips to Washington, he said, a White House limousine had met him at the airport. He observed: "But they never drive you *back* to the airport when they're through with you. And that's the time it's hellish hard to find a taxi!"

His cat-and-mouse game with the White House over the Romanov documents, as portrayed by himself, is one of the most painfully drawn-out series of postponements and bureaucratic frustrations that has ever come to my attention. Much of it took place when the big presidential mansion on Pennsylvania Avenue was in the throes of the Watergate scandals. That may have had a lot to do with it, but it leaves much more to be explained.

Here is an abbreviated scenario of the long run-around, starting more than three years ago, as Mr. Bessell reported it:

A few weeks after Mr. Bessell's request to Dr. Kissinger, he was told by a Kissinger aide that a preliminary check of various government departments had uncovered no Romanov papers of any sort. A few more weeks later, Mr. Bessell was summoned to Washington by a phone call from a Kissinger aide and told that some Romanov papers had been found still encoded in an old White House safe. Some of them were thereupon decoded, Mr. Bessell was informed, and he was shown a sampling of the sheets. This was the first time that Mr. Bessell saw any of the so-called Chivers Papers.

"Who was the Kissinger aide you dealt with?" I asked.

"Oh, let's call him 'Miller'," Mr. Bessell replied. "I'd like to keep his identity out of it. 'Miller' isn't his name. He's a younger historian, an old friend and disciple of Henry's brought in to do a certain job on old documents."

Mr. Bessell was advised at the same time that an effort was being made to authenticate the Chivers Papers. At a later date he was told that the code used in the Chivers Papers, as well as the paper, typewriter and typewriter ribbon involved, checked with other messages received and typed at corresponding dates. Then a Kissinger aide reported that plans were being made to declassify the papers a few weeks thereafter and place them in the National Archives, but first there would be consultations with other governments. (This was in the spring of 1971.)

A short time later Mr. Bessell was given the opportunity to study more than one hundred sheets in the Chivers file in Washington and copy the most important ones. He was told that the Japanese had found comparable, but not duplicate, papers in which there were discrepancies of dates and locales; that the Russians and French had found nothing conclusive, and that the British wanted more time to search. He was assured that a tentative release date for the Chivers Papers would be set for some time that fall.

Bessell was told in the fall (1971), that the release date had been put off until January, 1972. He was told in January that the date had been postponed again because some of the material in the Chivers Papers was considered "dangerous." He was told in February, 1972 that President Nixon was drawing up an executive order which would define the national policy for declassifying all old federal documents, including the Chivers Papers. Following the public announcement of the President's order on March 8, 1972, he was told that the Chivers Papers would be released in June; then he was told in July that they would be released in the fall of 1972 and was told in the fall that they would be released in January, 1973. In January he learned that a final, definite date for the release had been set for March 31, 1973, and that other governments had been so notified. But in late March the release date was delayed once more. At that time he was shown the Lord Hardinge letter to King George V which set forth the escape route of Nicholas and three of his daughters from Odessa to Breslau in 1919.

CHAPTER 2

EMERGENCE OF
THE CHIVERS PAPERS

By 1972 this tantalizing sequence of postponed deadlines and new promises had begun to make me suspicious. I was being forced to take Bessell's word for everything; he hadn't asked me to join him on any of those trips to the White House. I had no independent corroboration that the Chivers Papers really existed anywhere, nor any supporting evidence that what Bessell had been telling me was true. I had no proof that he had ever been in the White House in his life. He had admonished me repeatedly not to make any inquiries there about the Romanov Case under pain of having the whole program cancelled.

"Any sign of leaks, any instances of nosing around," he said, "and they'll simply pull back the Chivers Papers for a few more years. They told me as much!"

Even so, I reflected, there must be some way of establishing that this fast-talking Englishman hadn't invented the story of his liaison with Dr. Kissinger and "Mr. Miller;" that he hadn't forged the Chivers Papers, hadn't dreamed up their imminent declassification, hadn't faked his trips to Washington and wasn't carrying out a well-integrated British Intelligence plot to lead the Americans on a wild goose chase for years to come.

I mulled the problem over for a week or more, and decided on a tactic which contained risks, but which promised to determine whether or not Peter Bessell had indeed been dickering with the White House on the Romanov rescue story.

My able but reluctant collaborator in the test was David Maness, Assistant Managing Editor of *Life* Magazine. At the time, in the spring of 1972, *Life* had about seven months more to go. Its editors had expressed interest in the Romanov story, and had signed me up to do an article on it when and if the Chivers Papers were released.

It was Dave Maness's feeling that my projected testing tactic might blow all chances for the release of the documents, and he may have been right. But from my point of view, if the tactic succeeded, we would have ended any doubt that the White House was holding the Romanov papers and that Mr. Bessell was telling the truth.

Consider the time frame. The White House was reeling from leaks of all sorts of ticklish stories to *The New York Times, Washington Post* and Jack Anderson's column. The President's staff, as well as Henry Kissinger, were in a hypersensitive mood about not being able to do, say or write anything of importance without having it appear in print somewhere a day or two later. I decided that their hypersensitivity provided precisely the right atmosphere for pulling a quick-reaction checkup on Bessell.

Here was the idea. Think up a few sophisticated questions that suggested but did not conclusively betray an inside knowledge of the Chivers Papers. Pop them in Washington, London and Tokyo in places where — if they were deemed sticky enough — they would be reported back around the circuit to Dr. Kissinger. If they didn't aggravate him, nothing more would be heard of them. But if they alarmed him as signs of another leak, then someone at the White House would raise cain with Bessell. He would raise cain with me — and we would all know that Bessell hadn't been stringing a long bow with me.

There was always the chance, of course, that Kissinger would raise a storm that we'd never hear about. Then nothing would be proved. It was simply a risk that had to be taken.

The plan was implemented almost simultaneously in the three different parts of the world. Mr. Maness directed the *Life* correspondent in Tokyo to ask the Japanese Foreign Ministry for biographical background on one of their secret agents of the World War I vintage, a certain Colonel "Kiyaki" (first name unknown). Kiyaki is cited in the Chivers Papers.

Mr. Maness directed a *Life* reporter in Washington to ask the State Department's personnel records section why all essential data were missing on Henry J. Palmer, U.S. Vice-Consul at Ekaterinburg in 1918.

Mr. Maness directed the *Life* correspondent in London to phone Sir Thomas Preston at his home in Norfolk and ask him two questions:

First, did Sir Thomas, when he was British Consul at Ekaterinburg, know the American diplomat-on-station, Henry J. Palmer? Sir Thomas, now in his eighties, responded that he knew Mr. Palmer very well and had been a guest in Palmer's house when his own quarters were endangered by the Bolsheviks.

Second, why, then, did Sir Thomas fail to mention him in his splendid book about those days in Russia, *Before the Curtain?* Sir Thomas answered that it was probably an oversight on his part.

We are not certain which of these questions hit a sensitive nerve in Washington, but at least two of them boomeranged back. The morning of the third day, Mr. Bessell phoned and urged me to come to his office. When I got there he told me that the White House had bawled him out unmercifully and threatened to ditch the whole business. I flashed a pale smile and reminded him that they had ditched us so often already that the threat was getting to be something less than fearsome.

"There have been leaks in London and Tokyo," he said, "and God knows where else!"

He accused me of being the sieve.

"In this case you're right," I said.

I explained why, at that point of the burgeoning débacle, I felt the time had come to test him for subterfuge.

He rose and studied the Fifth Avenue scene seven stories below. He remained silent for a long count. Finally he turned and said:

"You know, by now I guess you're right. To tell the truth I've often put myself in your place. I've wondered why you didn't do something drastic to check on what I've told you."

I shouldn't have been elated but I was. The results — whatever they were to cost — had convinced me that we weren't being suckered by a con man. I could see no way that Mr. Bessell could have gained any inkling of the leaks if his tales of a White House connection were spurious. I certainly had not told him in advance about those Washington-London-Tokyo queries. Neither had Dave Maness.

But it looked as if we were in real trouble. It also looked as if I had outsmarted myself.

On both sides of the Atlantic, Mr. Bessell had augmented his public identification with the "no-assassination" version by authoring an article, "The Escape of Czar Nicholas and Alexandra," in the international magazine, *East Europe,* once a publication of Radio Free Europe, now edited largely for a clientèle of diplomats and businessmen interested in foreign trade.

"I am satisfied beyond any reasonable doubt," he wrote in this article, "that the Russian Imperial Family, i.e., the last Czar, Nicholas II, his wife and children, were not, as has been long supposed, assassinated at Ekaterinburg in July 1918, or, for that matter, elsewhere at any other time.

"With the carefully camouflaged assistance of two or more of the then Allied governments, they escaped to a country of relative safety, where they lived under assumed names.

"The evidence for this exists in the files of several Western governments and it is time for it to be published. . . ."

Deeper in his article he elaborated on a pact which he later found to have materialized into a secret codicil in the Treaty of Brest-Litovsk. He wrote:

"The reason for wishing to maintain this distortion of facts is now clear. An understanding was reached between the Russian and German Governments at the time of the armistice between those two countries, and later during the negotiations which led to the peace treaty of Brest-Litovsk, that the Russian government would assist in providing a safe passage for the Russian Imperial Family to a place of relative security. This was at the demand of Kaiser Wilhelm of Germany. The understanding led to violent dispute among the Russian Bolshevik leaders and was a cause of disagreement between Lenin and Trotsky (who believed quite genuinely that they were assassinated). On the one hand, the Russians were in fear of a renewed German invasion, which was entirely possible at the time. On the other, they could not be seen to be showing mercy to the Czar, whom they had depicted as a tyrant whose despotic rule had wrought the misery of the Russian peoples, who, in turn, had given power to the new government."

This was surely a topsy-turvy literary exercise for a British agent! If he was, indeed, seeking to ingratiate himself further with the anti-assassinationists, he was also sailing directly against the tide of the British Establishment's statements on the Romanovs and putting his reputation on the line with the bankers.

With the furor over the leaks and the backlash from the *East Europe* piece, it seemed by midsummer, 1972 that the Bessell-White House romance was as soured as President Nixon's pre-Watergate ties with the men around him. The prospects looked very dark, indeed, for an early release of the Chivers Papers.

We were wrong. In a few days Mr. Bessell reported that tempers in the White House had simmered down as far as he was concerned. He said he had resumed negotiations with the evanescent "Mr. Miller" and that something might happen at an early date. (From what ultimately transpired, hindsight suggests that a White House decision to continue to confer with Mr. Bessell might have been deemed the proper Florentine torture for continuing to punish him by degrees.)

Tentative new dates for declassification came and went. One of them seemed so certain that Mr. Bessell asked me to go to Washington and put in my application at the National Archives, but only in general terms, for material that more or less equated with that in the Chivers Papers. I did so.

There were two more false starts in early September and late November, 1972. Then in the middle of January, 1973 Mr. Bessell brought welcome news. The White House, he said, had picked a date which it believed would stand up under hell and high water. That date was Saturday, March 31. Though more than two months off, he pointed out, it would give everyone interested, including ourselves and the BBC, a chance to prepare for the great occasion. Because of our initial spadework on the case, he said, we would be given an advance look at the full set of Romanov documents from forty-eight to thirty-six hours ahead of everyone else. He added that other governments were being informed of the release date.

Suffice it to say that everyone interested *did* prepare for the great occasion. Because *Life* had suspended publication, I got in touch with North American Newspaper Alliance (NANA), the international newspaper syndicate, and found them just as interested in the story as *Life* had been. I wrote a series of articles for NANA subject to the projected release date. In London, the BBC put together another hour-long documentary ready for the weekend of March 31, except for a "top" footage of a few minutes duration that was going to be flashed from Washington to London via satellite. Several days before March 31, Peter Bessell went to Washington from New York — or said he did — for a final pre-release conference at the White House. A complicated and closely-timed plan had been worked out by NANA to pick up the documents in Washington and rush them to New York.

Then came the bombshell. It arrived by phone from Bessell late the night before we were to pick up our set of the Chivers Papers.

"They've put off the release date indefinitely," he said.

I passed on the bad news to NANA. They relayed it to their clients all over the world. The feeling of letdown all around the circuit could have been no worse. At this point the Nixon White House, among those familiar with the matter, hit the indicator of absolute zero popularity. It stank of rot and treachery.

So at this juncture, if he hadn't been conning us all along, Peter

Bessell could have been forgiven if he had been seized by an excess of nausea accompanied by internal hemorrhage, loss of breath, fluttering heart and a growing doubt that he was still sane. He showed no sign of these aberrations, but he was obviously piqued, and so was I.

After all, it was my government, not his. By the time of the final, great nonmaterialization I was thoroughly ashamed of a White House that had gulled and misled Bessell (unless he had gulled and misled us) and the many Americans who had worked on the case for years — persons who had followed Bessell's adventures on their behalf. Unless he was a phony himself, I reflected, he had wasted a small fortune in time and money in his dealings with the White House. His reward was outrageous. The only explanation he had been given, he said, was that someone in high authority had deemed the documents "too dangerous" for disclosure at the time. More than two years of hemming and hawing had been consumed before that decision was reached, at the eleventh hour. And all this while, without a word to any of the Americans, the White House had been dealing with us through a British go-between — Peter Bessell.

Sidney Goldberg, executive editor of NANA, was spurred into action. He got Dr. Kissinger by phone and fired such questions at him as "Do you know Peter Bessell? What's the score about releasing those Romanov documents?"

All Henry Kissinger's skills in the art of parrying with newsmen were displayed on the other end of the telephone. Mr. Goldberg reported his answers along these lines: "Peter Bessell? . . . Peter Bessell? . . . the name does sound familiar. . . . Let's see, yes . . . yes I believe I may have met him several years ago when he came over from Britain as a member of a Parliamentary committee on East-West trade.

"But new Romanov documents? No, I never heard of them. If they existed I'm sure my staff would have told me about them, you can be sure of that. They all know of my interest in history."

In the context of the time and the sudden developments, I knew that I would have to look at the situation bifocally. I would have to consider (a) that Henry Kissinger was telling the truth and Bessell was playing a game, or (b) that Bessell was telling the truth and Kissinger was following the dictates of his conscience in preventing NANA from releasing a story that he or President Nixon wanted withheld.

It was clear that if Kissinger had admitted knowing Bessell, as well as being familiar with the Chivers Papers, he was enough of a well-scarred bureaucrat to know that Goldberg might need no more assurance than that to break the story. In studying Kissinger's track record with the press, it is notable that he has followed the principle that government secrets are nonexistent until they are ready for official release. He has been a member of the school which uses imagination to make that nonexistence seem plausible. Badly burned by such celebrated contradictions of his own words as the Pentagon Papers case *(New York Times)*, the Bangladesh briefings (Jack Anderson) and the Plumbers Investigation (testimony before Watergate panels about the versions of Young and Colson), Kissinger had learned with some others of the Nixon Administration to be a "creative denialist." That means you don't rely wholly on your own rejection of the truth of a story that you are asked about. You add a creative embellishment or two designed to shake the reporter's faith that he is anywhere near the right track. That way, you hope, he will abandon his tip as a bum steer. You never use the phrase, "no comment." It is far too suggestive of trying to duck a hot subject — thereby confirming that the subject is hot; thereby encouraging the reporter to stay on the trail.

(Kissinger's favorite method for dealing with the press is to provide unattributable "background" briefings. He does so generously and with evident relish. This, of course, is an ideal way of spreading one's own pet theories and interpretations without having to take responsibility for them. With a little bit of luck, the reader or listener will believe the "news" originated with the reporter.)

Such, then, could have been the motive for Kissinger's allusion to his staff knowing all about his interest in history — a quick flip designed to flag down Goldberg's zeal. He knew that he had to admit knowing Peter Bessell (records are kept of White House visitors). He had an additional headache, if Bessell's account was true. He couldn't very well appeal to the national security angles, a favorite resort of the Nixon Administration, if he conceded the existence of the Chivers Papers, for he knew that they had been shown on his own orders to a foreigner — a legal violation — and he could presume that Goldberg would realize it.

So the full burden of the denial would have to fall on the documents. *Ipso facto,* they didn't exist.

But suppose Henry Kissinger had been speaking the literal truth in everything he said to Sidney Goldberg?

Suppose that all of Bessell's accounts of his White House conferences and the declassification plans had been fairy tales from start to finish?

I knew there was a perfectly good chance that both these suppositions were valid. It was very obvious that I was in for a long-range sleuthing operation before I could pin down the answers. I would have to tackle problems which would have been self-solving or quite academic if the Chivers Papers had been released as expected. But now I would have to establish quite independently of Bessell (1) that he visited Kissinger's offices on numerous occasions; (2) that the Chivers Papers truly existed; (3) that Bessell had been allowed to see them and copy many of them; (4) that they had been discussed with several foreign governments, and (5) that long before March 31, 1973 some of those governments had been notified that the release would come on that date.

I must say, my earlier trepidations that Bessell might be an MI-6 spook, or even a CIA spook, returned to haunt me. I considered asking Tony Summers and Tom Mangold to see what they could do in London with their British Secret Service contacts to determine whether Bessell was one of their talented ghosts.

A couple of days after Mr. Goldberg's colloquy with Dr. Kissinger, I held a conference with Mr. Bessell in his office. I found him in a rueful mood but still plotting to outmaneuver bureaucratic resistance. I asked him if he would be willing to prepare an affidavit covering his experiences with the White House on the case. He said he would. We discussed its wording and agreed on a preliminary draft. He volunteered that he had been thinking about the matter in all his waking hours and had concluded that the best place to resume the hunt was back where he had started three years before, namely in the House of Commons. Already, he said, he had been in touch by phone with his old friend and colleague, Jeremy Thorpe, Liberal Party Leader in Commons (who had emerged from the first 1974 national election as commander of a rough balance of power between the Conservatives and the Laborites). Mr. Thorpe agreed to take up the Romanov Case, Mr. Bessell told me. Since Thorpe would soon be returning to London through New York from a vacation in the Bahamas, they would confer on the matter and I would have a chance to meet Thorpe. Bessell praised Thorpe highly. He recounted how he and his party leader had worked together for years in political campaigns and on party business in Parliament.

This suited me. I was glad to think that the British flank of the old Anglo-American Coalition on the Romanov Case was not going to atrophy while I tried my best to pin down the facts in the United States.

In my post-fiasco conference with Mr. Bessell, I took time to review carefully all the circumstances of the day more than a year before when a Kissinger aide at the White House had allowed him, according to his version of the story, to copy most of the Chivers Papers. Here is Mr. Bessell's description of the event reduced to essentials:

The time of this copying session came after previous visits during which he had been shown selected sheets from the Chivers file. At last, on "Copy Day," he was handed a bulky sheaf of more than one hundred sheets. They were mostly messages dated in 1918 and 1919. Some were only a few paragraphs long. Some ran to several pages. Each bore the same disclaimer, which is not unusual on government papers stored in the National Archives — or papers being prepared for storage there — "NO REPRESENTATION IS MADE AS TO THE ACCURACY, ORIGIN OR AUTHENTICITY OF THIS DOCUMENT."

Mr. Bessell said that he was given a couple of hours or so for his note-making. He saw right away, he asserted, that he would not be able to copy everything before he ran out of time. He would have to decide what message was crucial for word-for-word transcription, and what could be summarized in a few paragraphs. He decided that some of the first messages sent from Siberia in July, 1918 and some of the last sent in the ensuing midwinter were too vital to try to compress. On the other hand, messages covering two or three sheets without reporting more than administrative matters could be summarized in a few sentences. He marked the messages accordingly. He was provided with a typewriter, he said. He is a fast typist and went to work on his task with the full realization of how helpful it could be to a writer preparing a series of articles against the deadline of a release date that, at the time, seemed close at hand.

Messages of which he copied the full text he marked "Verbatim." Those he paraphrased he marked "Not Verbatim." When he was finished he turned back all the originals and returned to New York, he said. A few days later, on a xerox machine in his New York office, he made copies of the twenty sheets he had typed in Washington and gave me a set. It was understood all around that they were to be held for official release.

"Were any of those papers you worked from stamped as being classified?" I asked.

"No, not that I could see," he answered.

"There was no stamp on them like 'secret' or 'top secret' or 'confidential'?" I asked.

"No," he said, "there might have been something like that on the folder or envelope in which they were filed. If so, I didn't see it. Remember, these messages were originally sent in code to Secretary of State Lansing in 1918 and 1919. I suppose that in those days the highly restrictive manner in which they were handled by the code clerk was considered security enough. After being read by Secretary Lansing and President Wilson, I was told, they were locked in a safe."

Mr. Bessell is right, as far as I have been able to determine. In World War I days there was nothing like the modern system for the security designation of documents in the federal agencies. In compliance with current laws and regulations, classified documents nowadays must be stamped with their category of restrictiveness and bear the name of the official who so designated them. Though White House personnel undoubtedly regarded the papers shown to Mr. Bessell as "classified," apparently no one in the White House had gotten around to stamping them as such. In terms of the now-prevailing security laws, they were as much in the clear as the contents of today's newspaper. I regarded Mr. Bessell's responses in these areas as important in helping to shape our future course of action, and considered a possible suit against the Government for withholding of the papers in violation of the provisions of the Freedom of Information Act.

By that time I had studied Bessell's copies of the Chivers messages very carefully. There were two reasons why I doubted that he had forged them himself. In the first place, as familiar as he was with the case, he would have had to be more of an expert than he was on the allusions in the messages' time frame. There were too many cross references to incidents and personalities in the idiom of the times that he couldn't have invented. Second, many of the towns and villages mentioned in them appear in their Czarist names, and two or three are so small that they can only be found on very detailed maps of the period. I was quite sure he hadn't conjured up this bit of reality contrivance. After I received my set of the documents from him, we discussed this point about verifying the place names. He said he wouldn't know where to start looking in New York. I told him in what part of the New York Public Library the answers could be found — but that was after I had copies of the papers.

Of course, that doesn't mean he *couldn't* have forged them. And it certainly doesn't mean that the papers couldn't have been created by experts in MI-6 or the CIA. But there again, one would be at a loss to find a motive. It would be far more likely that if they or the KGB had gone in for forgeries about the end of the Romanovs, they would have followed a line which tried to make the "assassination" more convincing than it was.

CHAPTER 3

JEREMY THORPE

Just as Mr. Bessell had forecast, the gauntly handsome Right Honourable John Jeremy Thorpe showed up in New York in April, 1973. Bessell arranged a meeting between us. With his bemused eyes, his trim physique and his racy sense of humor pitched in an Eton accent, Mr. Thorpe is an impressive personage. He is a restless presence whose manner is friendly and disarming but emanates warning that its possessor has a low boring point and could bolt away in a second. I viewed him with curiosity. Here was the figure famous in Britain as the half-Irish paradox of a man who delighted in mimicking his adversaries, and whose heart bled for the world's underdogs while he strode around dressed to the gills in a waist-coat and fancy pants. Here was the acrobatic campaigner whose witty sallies and unorthodox stances had somehow won him the image of a sort of Parliamentary vagabond and poet who would have felt at home with François Villon on the streets of Paris. If, as I recalled, some members of the British press had expressed doubt that "Jeremy" had any truly sustained program about anything, others, I recalled, had come to his defense by pointing out that the avoidance of an in-depth platform was the only possible way of holding together a party whose fragments had as many different colorations as a bowl of minestrone soup, and whose main cohesive force had been a common feeling of nausea for Wilson and Heath. As one British correspondent had informed me, "If Jeremy had ever come up with an overriding set of principles to apply to all issues, he'd have blown his party to bits. He has had the genius to appeal to all malcontents by saying nothing to dash their hopes that he's for everything they are."

This was the man who had been leading the Liberals to more and more seats in the House ever since 1959 when he won his first election from North Devon at the age of thirty. His father, J. H. Thorpe, was an M.P. before him. His own professional training was as a barrister.

There should be little wonder why Jeremy Thorpe is thoroughly at ease with Americans. His parents decided to expose him to the atmosphere of New England by sending him to the Rectory School in Pomfret, Connecticut, before he went on to Eton and Oxford.

"I loved the place and I loved Connecticut," he told me. "I still have the fondest memories of it. It gave me an outlook that I hope I'll never lose."

He arrived in New York with his Austrian-born wife, Marion, then a comely bride of a few weeks. She was once a concert pianist. Before she was divorced from the Earl of Harewood she was the daughter-in-law of Princess Mary, better known as the Princess Royal. (Mr. Thorpe's first wife, Caroline, was killed in a car accident in 1970.)

With Mr. Bessell present, we conferred as a foursome at a very appropriate spot for a talk about the rescue of the Romanovs, an apartment overlooking the United Nations.

Mr. Thorpe said that his old friend Peter [Bessell] had gotten him interested all over again in the fate of the Russian Imperial Family. He explained that his forebears had spent a great deal of time in Russia and one of them — I think he said it was his father — had received a Czarist decoration. As a student, he said, the Romanovs had always interested him. He asked me a great many questions about my investigation, and seemed to know a lot about the subject. He said he planned to take up the Romanov Case in Parliament when he returned to London.

He certainly didn't dawdle. A few days after he was back in London, Mr. Thorpe tackled the Foreign Office about the Romanovs and reported to Bessell frequently by phone. He discovered that another M.P., Anthony Royle, Minister of State for Foreign Affairs in the Heath government, was intensely interested in the Romanov mystery. Mr. Royle, it turned out, two years before had started an investigation of his own when expressions of doubt about the "assassination" story filled the British newspapers in 1971. Mr. Royle had arranged for a new search to be made for pertinent documents in the classified files of both the Foreign Office and the Windsor Archives. He said the results had puzzled him. In every set of papers on the Romanovs in both repositories, several key letters or papers always seemed to be missing. It looked as if someone had gone through all the files, left certain circumstantial material untouched but removed all conclusive material. Mr. Royle readily admitted — Bessell said — that he and his staff had been in touch with the Americans on the subject of newly-found Romanov documents and, he volunteered, he was quite surprised when March 31, 1973 came and went without any sign of the declassification in Washington that he had been told to expect.

On May 14, 1973, Mr. Thorpe fired his first gun in the House of Commons where he tried to table two questions to Foreign Secretary Sir Alec Douglas-Home. One asked the Government to place the Lord Hardinge letter which Mr. Bessell had copied in the White House, in the Commons library. The other asked what communication the Foreign Office had in the past year "with any persons or departments of government in Washington regarding the rescue of Czar Nicholas II."

Mr. Thorpe promptly encountered the same kind of "tabling trouble" which had greeted Mr. Bessell's questions in 1970, though the technicality cited was new. Mr. Thorpe's queries were ruled out-of-order on the ground that they dealt with past history. But the newsmen in the House who asked Mr. Thorpe to elaborate on what was behind his efforts were soon able to determine that the longtime enemy of government secrecy had launched a campaign on the Romanov Case which he was going to continue. Though he declined to reveal the contents of the Lord Hardinge letter, he said:

"The mystery of the Czar's fate is yielding up new secrets. The assassination version is increasingly open to doubt. Lord Hardinge of Penshurst was Permanent Under Secretary at the Foreign Office — but his letter was a private document. I believe it to be in the possession of the British or United States Governments, and that it points firmly to the conclusion that, in fact, the Czar escaped from Russia accompanied by the Grand Duchesses Olga, Tatiana and Marie. There is now growing interest in Washington as well in this fascinating historical issue."

Reuter's, AP and UPI sent out fulsome despatches about Thorpe's moves, and most newspapers and news magazines around the world published at least one of these stories. Several Sunday newspapers developed the theme into large features and it soon became clear to members of the Anglo-Saxon diplomatic establishments that Thorpe had barely begun his uncovering activities. The stories undoubtedly alerted those interested parties who were opposed to divulgement, and who hadn't been alerted already, that they had better use what influence they could in government circles to block the declassification.

During the summer recess of Parliament, Mr. Royle kept assuring Mr. Thorpe — according to Mr. Bessell — that the British and U.S. Governments were working on a mutually agreeable date for the release. Later in the fall, after Dr. Kissinger had been confirmed as Secretary of State, Mr. Royle told Mr. Thorpe, Mr. Bessell said, that Kissinger had "no objections" to an early date for a joint declassification by both Governments. Thorpe was given the impression that it would come very soon.

It didn't come soon enough to suit him. He waited many weeks more, then decided to take the bull by the horns by publishing the text of the Lord Hardinge letter and accusing one or more governments of withholding more pertinent data about the Romanovs. Before he could do so, however, things began to happen to him. He had to leave the country for a protracted period as a member of a parliamentary committee making a foreign survey. Then someone started a run on a savings institution of which Thorpe was a director. Emergency efforts to save it, though successful, demanded most of his time for weeks. Finally, Britain experienced a series of misfortunes — an outbreak of strikes, an energy crisis, a three-day work week and a dissolution of Parliament for a new national election. All provided a grim backdrop against which any political leader fussing over what happened to the Romanovs in 1918 could expect little more than public ridicule.

New obstacles also seemed to bedevil the activities of Mr. Thorpe's old friend and fellow Liberal, Peter Bessell. He had arranged for a British bank to buy a large tract of land in lower Westchester County, New York. The amount of money involved was several million dollars. The deal was all set; all it needed to become a binding contract was the routine approval of officials of the Bank of England who monitored the flow of British capital abroad in compliance with the export regulations of the Heath government. That approval never came, although for months there was no hint of a disapproval. The word from the Bank of England was that the sanction undoubtedly would be granted, but that papers on the case were piled up with dozens of others that had proliferated because of sticky situations which had developed over adverse trends in the balance of payments and dollar exchange. Month after month passed with no results. Twice Mr. Bessell flew to London and made personal appearances at the Bank of England in the hope of clearing the transaction. Each time he was told to be more patient; that the approval would probably materialize shortly.

There is small chance that Bessell dissimulated about this. I saw most of the papers and correspondence, and was well acquainted with the would-be American sellers. Ultimately I was told that the promised British source of capital grew weary of waiting and that Mr. Bessell turned to other bankers in Switzerland and Belgium.

The circumstances of Bessell's final days here are still unknown to me. The last I heard from him was some time around the Christmas holidays in 1973. He called to say that Jeremy Thorpe had set a date about two weeks off for resuming his public maneuvers on the Romanov Case. Shortly thereafter he flew to Los Angeles to confer on another real estate venture.

That winter conditions in the United Kingdom steadily worsened in a scene of strikes, brownouts and shortened work weeks, and Prime Minister Heath finally asked Queen Elizabeth to dissolve Parliament (Feb. 8, 1974) for another national election.

In Los Angeles, in January, 1974, Mr. Bessell kept at least one of his business appointments. A few days later, when the man he met there tried to reach him, he couldn't be found. The man called the New York office and was told by Bessell's daughter, Paula, that she had no idea where her father was.

A few days later the New York office was closed; then the London office was closed.

What happened to him?

Was he demolished by the British Establishment?

Was his American visa lifted by order of the State Department?

Or was he simply caught in the financial crunch which made the winter of 1973–74 such a bitter memory for many international brokers and investors?

On June 14, 1974, the *London Express* published the following story by John Harrison about Peter Bessell under the headline, "Missing ex-MP riddle":

NEW YORK Thursday: Pauline Bessell, wife of former Liberal MP Peter Bessell, talked tonight about the heartbreak of finding her husband missing from home, the enormous debts he left behind — and her fears for his safety.

"He left a letter the day he went," said Mrs. Bessell, a mother of two. "It was a sad note but very sweet. Sweet because he said he was worried about how people might treat me and the children after he disappeared, and sad because, from the way he wrote, he was obviously very tired and ill."

Mr. Bessell, who moved to New York four years ago to make his fortune in property financing, disappeared from his New York apartment in January of 1974.

Mrs. Bessell said of the five-month mystery: "I think he's probably somewhere in South America. He left no clues as to where he was going. He just said he was tired and thought it would be the best thing.

"He knows he has left debts behind. He has a conscience and I know he's thinking about what happened. We were a very happy family and Peter and I were very happily married. I hope one day he contacts me."

Mr. Bessell, aged 52, Liberal M.P. for Bodmin, Cornwall from 1964 to 1970, ran two companies based in New York — Peter Bessell U.S.A. Inc., and 20th Century Securities. He recently sold his house in Looe and closed his London office in Pall Mall.

His solicitors and accountants in London and Plymouth had been trying to contact him for some time when, on October 2, 1974, The *Daily Mail* of London ran a short story to the effect that Bessell's daughter had traced her father to Venezuela. She was quoted as saying that "we are all trying to sort things out and we want him back."

CHAPTER 4

CLUES FROM THE C.I.A.

So much for the Britons. The Americans were moving even slower.

By the middle of January, 1974 it was clear that the American operation would have to be conducted on three levels, all of which would probably require a separate cast of characters with their own special connections. The task shaped up something like this:

(1) Confirmation that Mr. Bessell had visited the White House and Kissinger's office would require help from persons who had friendly access to receptionists, secretaries, security guards, Secret Service agents and drivers working for the White House limousine unit. For such a checkout, furthermore, photographs of Bessell could be helpful to refresh memories. Fortunately I had some snapshots of him.

(2) Confirmation that the Chivers Papers existed would require one or more persons who had no trouble reaching President Nixon, Dr. Kissinger or one of the high Presidential aides.

(3) Confirmation that the British Foreign Office had been informed about the Chivers Papers and the Lord Hardinge letter in all likelihood would need the services of high BBC officials if

Jeremy Thorpe, Tony Summers or Tom Mangold couldn't swing it. I would also have to try to determine whether some of my other associates in London didn't have a personal acquaintance with Tony Royle in the Foreign Office, or with someone of comparable stature.

Finding and briefing the right people for these assignments consumed most of a month. It was an interminably stretched-out process. It entailed dozens of late-at-night phone calls and a number of before-breakfast chats with London. Nothing seemed to go right. By the middle of February, Parliament was dissolved, and persons like Jeremy Thorpe were hopping all over England talking to voters outside pubs, post offices and factories. Henry Kissinger was cavorting in his jet from Mexico to the Arab capitals.

By the end of March, after Jeremy Thorpe had refused Prime Minister Heath's offer to join a coalition government, and Prime Minister Wilson was back at Britain's shaky helm, it seemed to me that nothing had been accomplished at all. I had received no feedbacks whatsoever from the teams working in Washington and London. What gains there were had issued from unexpected directions. Though I was very late in getting the news, it came to my attention that the Conservative Republican, Rep. John M. Ashbrook of Ohio, had of his own accord incorporated the matter of the Romanovs' rescue in his running battle with the State Department over old documents being withheld from Congress. He had taken up the issue on the House floor. His speech with related correspondence appeared in the *Congressional Record.*

Then I crossed the path of Senator Claiborne Pell, the Liberal Democrat from Rhode Island. My guide in this encounter was an old friend and Romanov buff who is one of Pell's constituents — Dr. Hannibal Hamlin of Providence, a well-known brain surgeon. I learned that Senator Pell, a member of the Foreign Relations Committee, had been trying for years to find out more about the missions performed a half century ago by his stepfather, Commander Hugo William Koehler. Commander Koehler was a Naval Intelligence agent in the World War I era. He served on occasions as a State Department special agent. His name had come to me through an associate, Mr. Jon Speller of New York City. Mr. Speller had learned that at least three Naval officers acting as secret agents could have had a lot to do with rescuing the Romanovs and escorting them from the Ekaterinburg area to Odessa. They were, he was told, Newton A. McCully, Sergius M. Riis and Hugo W. Koehler, all of whom had received high American and Czarist decorations after World War I. So it was in pursuing the Koehler lead that I met Senator Pell.

The Senator became interested from the start. He chairs several subcommittees which deal with documents, archives, history, declassification and the Library of Congress. On March 20, 1974, he sent a letter of inquiry about Koehler and the Chivers Papers to Secretary of State Henry Kissinger. Three weeks later he was favored with a reply. Kissinger had turned over the chore of answering Pell to an underling, Linwood Holton, Assistant Secretary for Congressional Relations. The reply stated in part as follows:

"Neither the Department of State nor the National Archives has in its custody any group of papers termed the 'Chivers File.' We have no knowledge of any hidden papers in American records that would prove the escape of the Tsar or any member of his family. Moreover, we find it hard to imagine why anyone in the United States Government would have an interest in concealing such facts, or that such sensational information could have been successfully hidden throughout all the upheavals and political changes which have taken place in Europe in the 55 years since 1918.

"The records of the Department of State for this period of history have been open to the public in the National Archives for many years. . . ."

A total deception! (As we found out later.) Completely omitted from this letter was any reference to the following facts:

For years before the CIA was formed in 1947, the State Department had its own little CIA with its own coterie of secret agents. It was operated by the department's Chief Special Agent, who played a low profile role. His title rarely showed on the personnel rosters or departmental phone books. You had to know his name to find him.

When Congress passed the National Security Act of 1947, and created the Central Intelligence Agency, the CIA scraped the barrel of talent in the Federal agencies for qualified sleuths and secret agents. It grabbed Robert Bannerman, Chief Special Agent of State at the time, and when he was transferred to the CIA he took his files with him. Automatically they ceased to be State Department files and became CIA files. Thus it is to the archives of the CIA in Langley, Virginia, that the turn in the road now leads to all the old secret operations — to the files on Newton McCully, Sergius Riis, Hugo Koehler, Roy C. Woods and a host of others.

The public, the Congress, the world at large are being sedated and misled by the bureaucracy supported by American taxpayers. For Linwood Holton's letter to Pell is a bland stereotype of all the responses State has made in the last few years to questions about the Romanovs posed by senators, congressmen, historians and others. Note that Holton wrote that "Neither the Department of State nor the National Archives has in its custody. . . ." but makes no reference to the 1947 transference of those old State Department Chief Special Agent files to CIA, or to the fact that the CIA might have them in *its* custody.

If Linwood Holton is as uninformed as his letter would have him appear, then he can hardly be accused of duplicity. But there are others in State who knew about the transference of the Chief Special Agent's files to CIA and could have supplied Senator Pell with the lead. They chose not to do so. I visited State a few weeks after the Holton letter was sent to Pell. A spokesman confirmed the facts about Bannerman, but only after being challenged. He also volunteered the information that several persons collaborated on the drafting of the reply to Pell. That is probably why it took them so long. It turned out to be technically accurate but substantially false, like so many other recent utterances of the executive branch.

The letter also would have its recipient believe that no such thing as a "Romanov file" ever existed in the Department of State since it isn't there now and isn't in the National Archives. I discussed this issue with the spokesman. He reiterated the nonexistence theory. When I reached in a folder and pulled out a photocopy of a State Department document in the National Archives, duly initialed by several officials, and clearly marked "Romanov File," the spokesman replied:

"Oh, that doesn't mean a thing! An executive can mark a paper or a file or anything he wants to. The true designation of the file is that number there, right on the margin — see it?"

I saw it. I also saw the words "Romanov File." I tried to remind him that it was more likely to be by words rather than numbers that people wrote, spoke and otherwise tried to communicate with each other.

Just to clinch the point, a colleague tracked down one of the State Department officials whose signature "RFK" appears on this Aug. 25, 1927 document close to the words "Romanov File." He is Robert F. Kelley, former head of the Russian (Eastern European Affairs) section of State who — though retired — still receives assignments from the Government. He refused to discuss the Romanov case but readily identified his signature on the document.

"I'll tell you this," he said. "If I wrote 'Romanov File' there, as I obviously did, you can bet there was a Romanov File."

Mr. Kelley's residence is in Washington.

On May 28, 1974 I mailed a two-page letter to CIA Director William E. Colby. In it I asked his permission to study the files which Mr. Bannerman had taken with him to the agency in 1947, more especially those on McCully, Riis, Koehler and Woods. I enclosed a copy of a letter from Senator Pell expressing a similar interest in the records. I must say I enjoyed thinking about Mr. Colby's possible reactions to my letter and his probably puzzled deliberations with his aides. Some of those aides, but not many, may have been born before the Romanovs were taken to Ipatiev House. Others without doubt were first laid in their bassinets years later. I could imagine any one of them exclaiming: "Nineteen Eighteen, Nineteen Nineteen! — Good God, what has all that got to do with Arab oil or Cyprus?"

I resigned myself to a long wait for any kind of a response from Mr. Colby. It was during the doldrums of this long wait that there were a few interesting developments.

One was a sign that the Soviet Union had heard about the Chivers Papers and had been worried into countermeasures. I received a translator's report on a lengthy series of articles on the last years of czarism appearing in the Soviet literary monthly *Zvesda*. It followed the conventional, anti-imperialistic line up to the days of the "assassination." Then it devoted a great deal of time to attacking Americans who were advancing the theory that the Romanovs were rescued. It singled out for scorn Robert Speller, President of Robert Speller & Sons, publisher of Mrs. Eugenia Smith's *Anastasia*, which said nothing about a general rescue, and numerous other volumes by European writers and statesmen. The *Zvesda* series termed Mr. Speller a CIA agent, which was news to his friends, if not to him.

No doubt the *Zvesda* series was a signal of some sort. Many of the installments ran to novelette length. They carried the byline of an unknown writer whom Western students of the Soviet literary stables surmised to be a KGB ghost. The articles represented a large investment in time, ink and paper. For a nation which has largely ignored the Romanovs since the Revolution, they marked the first indication that Russian scholars in the West could recall of any great amount of attention — uncomplimentary as it was — being lavished on the former residents of Tsarkoe Selo by the Communist literary establishment. The net effect of the series was to rebury the Romanovs deeper than ever. But why — if their graves were undisturbed, if they were truly deceased — this extra effort to inter them all over again?

In Soviet Russia very little propaganda is unleashed by accident. Thus the *Zvesda* series could well be interpreted as a token of the pressure vented on Henry Kissinger after the word filtered out that he was thinking of releasing the Chivers Papers. (The reader may not need to be reminded that membership in the Russian Orthodox Church is more than twice as large as membership in the Soviet's Communist Party. The Czar was head of the church. Proof of the survival of Nicholas and his family could be highly embarrassing to the bureaucratic Red heirs of Lenin and Trotsky. It could produce a backlash among devout church members. It would show that the Russian government had consistently lied for years about what happened at Ekaterinburg. It would inform the congregations that they had been praying quite erroneously over the decades for seven nondeparted souls.)

There were two other developments in the long wait of 1974. Several British scholars who are experts on Lord Hardinge were given a chance to study the text of the letter which Jeremy Thorpe publicized in England — but without disclosing its contents. The scholars disagreed over certain fine points. But the time they devoted to the study fleshed out in greater depth and color the events covered in the letter, and the relationship between its author and the British Royal Family. This, in turn, led to a new horizon — Bulgaria.

The Lord Hardinge letter puts Bulgaria on the Romanovs' itinerary after they were rescued and placed aboard a British ship at Odessa in February, 1919. This conforms with the times and places given in the Chivers Papers. Bulgaria provided a new direction to think about. None of the American team had realized that young King Boris III of Bulgaria — though the scion of a Roman Catholic family — was actually a member of the Orthodox Church. None of us had taken time to note how close Bulgaria's seaports on the Black Sea are to Odessa. Far more important, none of us had bothered to discover that Nicholas II, through an odd set of circumstances, was King Boris's godfather through vows given in the Orthodox Church, and that Boris was under heavy obligation to render him aid and comfort.

These revelations plunged us into days of research on Bulgarian history. With the bountiful help of persons close to the Bulgarian Orthodox and Russian Orthodox Churches, they added a new chapter to this book. They helped to make the long wait worthwhile.

CHAPTER 5

DECLASSIFICATION DELAYED

Late in June, 1974 the signals began to spell a hint that the era of great vacillation was over — that the almost incredible years of federal obduracy about the Romanov documents were drawing to an end.

I finally received an answer to my letter to the CIA about a month after I mailed my questions. Yes, the agency *had* found certain documents that I had asked for, wrote Angus MacLean Thuermer, Assistant to CIA Director Colby. They concerned "the activities of Sergius M. Riis during the period of your interest" (1918 and 1919). In an extremely helpful response to my queries, Mr. Thuermer also told me where I could find further information about Newton A. McCully's service in Naval Intelligence.

The documents on Riis were still classified, Mr. Thuermer explained. They had been sent to "the originating agencies for declassification review" and he stated that he would notify me "when decisions had been reached" or "if other relevant material should come to light."

Up to the moment of his writing, he noted, they hadn't found anything about the other two Americans, Koehler and Woods.

I was not very hopeful that "the originating agencies" (State and Navy?) would approve the release of the Riis papers, but the communication from Thuermer confirmed that the Government held data on Riis which — at least fifty-five years after the services rendered — remained in the secret category. There was no clue in Thuermer's letter about the nature of the Riis material, but his letter to me completely contradicted the text and spirit of the State Department's letter to Senator Pell.

At about the same time that the CIA responded, I got a little encouraging feedback from the White House. A friend of mine who is also a friend of J. Fred Buzhardt Jr., then President Nixon's counsel, had agreed to take up the subject of the Chivers Papers with him. Two weeks and two days after the compact was made, my friend reported that he had had a preliminary session with Mr. Buzhardt about the matter and the reply was threefold: a) Mr. Buzhardt knew of Mr. Richards and "his thesis;" b) Mr. Richards should be reminded of the rules vis-à-vis state secrets, and c) Mr. Buzhardt was going to take up the subject of the Romanov Case with Henry Kissinger as soon as Kissinger "lit" for any length of time.

It so happened that June, 1974 also marked a salient in the career of Dr. Kissinger. It was the month he received euphoric accolades for his arduous and successful negotiations leading to the disengagement of Syrian and Israeli forces. It was also the month when he returned to the capital of his adopted country to receive jarring treatment from some of those correspondents who, up to then, had spared him the caustic attacks they had launched against President Nixon and other favorite Watergate targets. In a study of American diplomatic tactics that led to the signing of the Vietnam agreement in January, 1973, Tad Szulc described Kissinger's methods in an article in *Foreign Policy* magazine. *New York Times* columnist Anthony Lewis reviewed Mr. Szulc's findings as follows:

"Mr. Kissinger is inevitably the main focus of this article. His negotiating techniques are laid bare. To a notable extent, they amount to deception: telling each side what it wants to hear. In Vietnam, the technique failed in the end — after a last virtuoso display of two-faced tactics."

This echoed a complaint which the *Times'* then Vice President and columnist, James Reston, forwarded from diplomatic circles in Paris — that Kissinger told the French one thing, the British another, the West Germans another, and nobody knew what to believe.

In June the *Times* also ran a page one exclusive to the effect that Kissinger had called the shots in extending wiretaps beyond mid-1969 on his National Security Council aide, Morton I. Halperin, in conflict with Kissinger's testimony before the Senate Foreign Relations Committee in September, 1973. This bore out testimony made public earlier by a federal judge from an affidavit given by Charles W. Colson, a former Presidential counsel, that "Dr. Kissinger was even more alarmed over the leaks [of the classified Pentagon Papers] than the President."

Questioning Dr. Kissinger on the same subject of his role in the wire tapping of aides, Washington correspondent Clark Mollenhoff gave the Secretary of State a very bad time on what was slated as a triumphant press conference after Kissinger's return from his mediation miracles between Syria and Israel. It is not often that the performance of one reporter in a press conference becomes the subject of another's laudatory account. In this case, however, the scheduled love feast for Kissinger was transformed into a love feast for Mollenhoff by Mary McGrory, the Washington press corps' Deadly Nightshade of the Distaff Side. She wrote:

"Clark Mollenhoff, who has the build of a tank and the voice of a hog caller, rode down all other plaints of 'Mr. Secretary,' and roared at him (Kissinger):

" 'What you have engaged in here is a pattern of evasion and failure to recollect . . . that we have seen over a period of weeks. I wonder why you cannot answer the direct question: Did you have any direct role in initiating wiretaps on your subordinates?'

"Kissinger, distraught, escalated the number of hours he had testified before the Senate Foreign Relations Committee to nine.

" 'You still haven't answered,' Mollenhoff bellowed. 'Did you go to John Mitchell?'

"The Secretary faltered, stumbled, repeated himself: he had supplied, his office had supplied . . . the names . . .

" 'Did you make a recommendation?' asked Mollenhoff, who worked briefly in the White House and knows its ways.

" 'No direct recommendation,' Kissinger rejoined lamely. 'I think this is a press conference, and not a cross-examination.'

"He was wrong. It was a cross-examination, and it could even be the first of several for the outraged idol."

This would seem to be an uncharitable welcome home, indeed, for a man who had burned the midnight oil for days on end in his search for peace in the Middle East. But it was, in its way, a come-uppance for one of the most elusive personages in Washington. For more than two years of the coverage of Watergate by the media, Henry Kissinger had remained Nixon's white knight, unscathed by all but a few lonely detractors. But now, as he stood flustered in the glare of the TV cameras, it was clear that the process of his de-immunization from rough handling by his interrogators was well under way. Only a small portion of the public could have realized that the words and visage of Mr. Mollenhoff bore disturbing ghosts for Dr. Kissinger. The two had tangled before during the former's brief and unhappy tour of duty in the White House as ombudsman for the citizenry. So nettled by the encounter was the Secretary of State, that in a tense and hastily-organized press conference a few days later in Salzburg he threatened to resign if the Senate Foreign Relations Committee didn't clear him of the charges implied in Mr. Mollenhoff's questions.

I took no pleasure in Dr. Kissinger's discomfiture. Anyone who has worked as hard in the nation's interests, even though his methods may be questionable, is entitled to an off day. But for someone like myself who had come to disbelieve in Kissinger's credibility, as the procrastination over the Chivers Papers dragged into years, it was comforting to know that his views were being questioned by such good minds as Szulc, Lewis, Reston, Mollenhoff and McGrory. Implicit in this thought was the recollection of the sharp variance in facts about the U.S. agents in Russia in 1918 and 1919 which Senator Pell received as a result of his letter to Kissinger, and the response given on the same subject by the CIA.

No one can blame the peripatetic doctor for suppressing the Chivers Papers after first deciding that such ancient documents should be passed into the public domain. The President himself could have reversed Kissinger's judgment about it. But no excuse can be found for either Nixon or Kissinger misleading Peter Bessell and the large group of Americans interested in the case into believing, month after month, year after year, that declassification was just around the corner.

Sources of the suppressive influences on the White House remain only guesses. Bankers here or abroad may have exerted the pressure. It may have come from the Romanovs' relatives, the Royal Family of England. It may have come from the Russian Orthodox Church which, as the organization once headed by Nicholas II, reportedly has hopes of ultimately receiving funds still being held by banks to his account.

It may also have come from Columbia Pictures. There was a rumor that someone in Columbia pleaded with the White House not to release the Chivers Papers lest the divulgement complicate Columbia's negotiations for the sale of their "Nicholas and Alexandra" production to a TV network. The movie has the Romanovs assassinated at the end.

But until evidence emerges to the contrary, a good hunch as to the origin of the phrase uttered to Peter Bessell about the Chivers Papers at the White House — "They're too dangerous" — is the Kremlin. There isn't enough space here to cite all the reasons why the withholding of the Chivers Papers by the Nixon Administration could have been another of those kindnesses which Americans are always being asked to render the Soviets to keep the scales of détente in balance with their views. The formula is now familiar. It applies to both tangibles and intangibles: more and more American contributions at lower and lower rates of interest.

This hunch earned further validation in my mind when, in rapid succession during late June, 1974, our detective work in London and Washington was rewarded by affirmative reports. Three out of four points of verification were resolved in Peter Bessell's favor. There was a breakdown in the mechanics of trying to substantiate a fourth point. With the resources at our disposal it seemed possible that it would take months to run it out.

We decided it was not essential. Three out of four was a good endorsement of the fact that the Chivers Papers were in the Government's possession and were regarded seriously. Taken together, all three overwhelmingly ratified the same concept. I am not going to be more explicit. To do so could cost several persons their jobs.

But glancing backward — from what I know now — Dr. Kissinger's denial to Sidney Goldberg that he knew anything about the Chivers Papers can be equated in value to the statement he had prepared for President Nixon's voicing which upheld the non-involvement of U.S. forces in Cambodia.

In closing this preamble, it would seem almost sacrilege to turn to the Chivers Papers without mentioning two of the many, long-available bits of circumstantial evidence that have been sleeping through the years with endorsements of the Chivers scenario.

One, of course, is the account given by Nicholas's old valet, Terenti Ivanovich Chemodurov, describing how the Romanovs escaped under cover of the murder of two members of their entourage. The Chivers Papers tell the same story.

Another is the extraordinary case of Roy C. Woods, the former Illinois Assistant State's Attorney. American novelist Kenneth Roberts encountered Mr. Woods in Danzig and Warsaw in 1923 and wrote several pages in his memoirs about Woods' secret plane trips from Warsaw into the Polish countryside in the course of negotiations with the Czar's daughter, the Grand Duchess Tatiana. According to Roberts in his book, *I Wanted to Write,* Mr. Woods was helping her plan a trip to the United States — five years after her supposed "murder" — in which she was going to bring a treasure in jewels and paintings by such masters as Van Dyck, Rembrandt, Holbein and Titian which had been smuggled out of Russia. Roberts described the flamboyant lawyer from the midwest as an "elegantly-dressed, Charles Dana Gibson-ish American" who was rolling in money and used "a superior grade of perfume and carried a pearl-handled revolver in his hip pocket."

Our search for Mr. Woods started in 1970. We gave him up as long since dead after tracing his retirement trail through communities in Illinois and Minnesota. But we were wrong.

In the spring of 1974, Mr. Woods proved himself very far from dead. He was tracked down in Scottsdale, Arizona, by a relentless member of the American research team, Chicago lawyer M. Robert Samborski. In good health, in his middle nineties, Mr. Woods refused to talk about his adventures in Poland in 1923 beyond saying, "I was on a special mission for Secretary of State Charles Evans Hughes." Up to the moment of the interview in the Arizona sun he had never read, he said, what Roberts had written about him. He didn't know that the divulgement of his secret had been a matter of public record for a quarter of a century!

Another substantiation of the Chivers documents also has been in type for many years — but in French. It is a portion of the Nicholas A. Sokolov Report on the "assassination" as first published in Paris. The portion was dropped from the later German and Russian editions. It tells how a group of influential Cossacks, Whites and Monarchists in the Ukrainian city of Kiev were forewarned on July 5 or 6, 1918 that a staged assassination of Nicholas would take place between July 16 and 20; that the news of it would be false, but that they should help spread it around in the interests of Nicholas's safety.

Judge Sokolov reported that Prince Dolgorukov testified as follows:

"I recall very well that on the 5th or 6th of July, 1918, Bezak [an official] informed me by telephone that Alvensleben [Count Hans-Bodo von Alvensleben, the Kaiser's personal contact with the Cossack commander] had just come to visit him to give him some important news. I went to Bezak's . . . Alvensleben told us that the Emperor Wilhelm wished to rescue the Emperor Nicholas at all costs, and had taken measures to that end. . . .

"He forewarned us that between the 16th and 20th of July we would learn that the Emperor had been put to death. He also forewarned us that, like the rumors current in June concerning the death of the Emperor, this news would be false, but that it was necessary to disseminate it in the interests of the Emperor himself.

He asked us to keep this conversation secret, and to let others believe, when the moment came, that we were convinced of the Emperor's death. On the 18th or 19th of July the newspapers in Kiev announced that the Emperor had been put to death in Ekaterinburg and that the Imperial Family had been removed to a safe place. I was astounded, I assure you, by the manner in which Alvensleben proved to have such advance information."

The churches of Kiev soon filled with communicants praying for the soul of the former Czar. Funeral services were held for him.

"There was no delay in the spread of the news," Prince Dolgorukov added, stating that Alvensleben had wept during the funeral service. "Bezak and I were amazed to see the facility with which this man played his role."[*]

It's a role that has been played over the years by a few others, mostly Russians, who have known of the rescue all along but felt restrained as a matter of honor to keep it secret. Like Alvensleben, they have learned to weep on demand.

[*]See pages 87 and 88 of John F. O'Conor's study of the Sokolov investigation (Refer Bibliography).

TELEGRAM RECEIVED.

CSD   GREEN

FROM

INDEX BUREAU
REC'D

DEC. 6 1918

DEPT OF STATE

Rome

Department of SDated Dec. 4,1918

DEC 6 - 1918 Recd. 5th., 9:17 p.m.

DIV. OF NEAR EASTERN AFFAIRS
(RUSSIA)

Secretary of State

Washington

2443, Routine, December 4, 6 p.m.

For your confidential information. I learned that in highest quarters here it is believed that the Czar and his family are all alive. Paris informed.

NELSON PAGE.

HAO

On December 4, 1918, when the Romanovs were about to travel from the Ekaterinburg area to Odessa, U.S. Ambassador Nelson Page sent word to Washington that "highest quarters" in Rome believed that the Imperial Family "are all alive." This message was found in 1969 in the National Archives. [Xerox of a State Dep't. telegram.]

PART II

THE ESCAPE

AGAIN REPORT CZAR TO BE STILL ALIVE

Grand Duke Cyril Given as Authority for Story That Officer Was Shot Instead.

HIS FAMILY ALSO LIVING

News Said to Have Been Conveyed in Letter from Ex-Autocrat's Daughter Tatiana.

LONDON, Jan. 8. (British Wireless Service.)—According to a story sent by a special correspondent of The Morning Post at Archangel—which it is necessary to treat with reserve—the former Emperor of Russia is still alive. The correspondent telegraphs:

"A friend of mine, Prince M——, who has just arrived here from Petrograd, informed me that he had a long talk with Grand Duke Cyril on Nov. 18. The Grand Duke told him that he had just received a letter from Grand Duchess Tatiana, daughter of the Emperor, who wrote that the Empress and her daughters were still alive and that the Emperor had not been shot.

"The Bolshevist officer who was ordered to carry out the sentence of death told the Emperor that it was a matter of indifference to him who was shot. He had orders to produce a corpse—bullets in the head of a victim would make identification impossible.

"Count T——, who was present at the conversation, offered to sacrifice himself, saying he considered it was his duty to lay down his life for his sovereign. The Emperor protested vehemently, but was overrruled by Count T—— and the officer. The Emperor escaped, but no one knows where he is at the present time.

"Dr. Botkin has also written to his sister to the effect that 'the greatest crime of the twentieth century has miscarried.'"

SAY EX-CZAR'S MOTHER GETS LETTERS FROM HIM

Polish Officers Report Former Dowager Empress Still Lives Near Livadia, Crimea.

WARSAW, Dec. 16. (Associated Press.) The mother of former Emperor [...] Livadia, in the Crimea, has been living near [...] letters every ten days purported to come from the former ruler, according to Polish officers who have arrived here from Sebastopol.

BELIEVES CZAR LIVES.

Russian Prince Thinks Royal Family Is Hidden in Northern Russia.

ROME, March 10 [...] talking to an interview [...] of a noble [...] a daughter [...] day in [...] still ext [...] wife [...] grand [...] He [...] The [...] twen [...] rmer [...] iard [...] cit [...] milk [...]

SAYS CZAR AND FAMILY ARE IN NEUTRAL LAND

Nephew of Skoropadski Asserts Their Whereabouts Is Known to Allied Government.

WARSAW, Dec. 21. (Associated Press.) There is no doubt that the Czar and his entire family are alive [...] position. Of this it was made to the correspondent today by Michael [...] of General Skoropadski, a nephew [...] escaped from the [...] who has just [...] trip to Petrograd, Polish [...] and Rovno [...] I cannot tell where the Czar is because he does not wish it, he added. He wants to be left alone [...] The whereabouts is known to an allied government [...]

Accounts [...] is in a neutral [...] and were [...] his murder [...] purposes and famine manufactured at [...] It is a truth money and time and [...] many officers to an [...] was [...] Among the [...] former [...] Count Tatishev, the officer [...] shot instead of military attache [...] describing the Czar [...] in the hands of the German Consul [...] who forwarded

In 1918, and in the '20s, a number of newspaper stories were printed to the effect that some or all of the Romanovs survived. These are from *The New York Times*.

CHAPTER 6

THE CZAR BECOMES A PARIAH

Few faces in history have come to mean so many things to different persons as the bearded, imperial visage of Czar Nicholas II. To some his face is the symbol of a classic regal martyrdom. To others it denotes a bland stupidity which was the principal cause of the bloody Russian Revolution. To still others, it conveys a sense of grand tragedy with some of the romantic overtones of a massacred saint or the murder of Julius Caesar: the untimely demise of an exalted personage in a world which had become impossible, incomprehensible or ungrateful.

To victims of the oppressive and dreaded Okhrana, the Czarist secret police, Nicholas represented the pampered, protected, prettied-up façade of a royal hypocrite who hid behind the moats of his palaces while his henchmen sucked the lifeblood of the masses and ruthlessly shot or jailed all protesters. To many devout members of the Russian Orthodox Church, however, Nicholas's features were only slightly less sacred than those of the Saviour Himself, for he was head of the church, and they believed that God had assigned the Czar the mission of carrying out His will on earth.

Outside Russia, to some monarchists his face was the apotheosis of a pitiful failure whose blind adherence to an autocratic code cost him his empire, lost Russia its centuries-old crown and launched a chain reaction against kings all over the world. To other monarchists it was the emblem of a man of unwavering faith and principle who was betrayed by his wartime allies and who, after his own country had been bled dry in helping to save the Western Powers, saw it stolen from him by a coterie of aristocratic traitors, foreign conspirators and agents of his own allies.

To the few who had enough rank in the pecking order of Czarist society to have known him socially, all replicas of Nicholas were reminders of a charming, gentle and not very bright personage who loved his family, who was uncomfortable in the endless ceremonials of his office, and who had a clear preference for his days in the country or cruising on his yacht, *Standart.*

His was a face which undoubtedly carried many other shades of meaning to others. Not the least of these could have been the case of those of his subjects for whom his image became the souvenir of a long trip taken from some distant part of his empire (it comprised more than one-seventh of the earth's land-surface) to St. Petersburg or Tsarskoe Selo just for a fleeting glimpse of it, and thereafter a cherished memory for years. To them its meaning became inseparable from the acutely personal experiences of a sacred pilgrimage. The high motives of the great figure they had gone to see were as unquestionable as the high motives which had inspired the trip, and so the two thoughts stayed fused through the mists of time. Reports of the assassination of the Imperial Family only served to hallow Nicholas's charisma in the minds of such persons. Their feeling of heartache about the Romanovs was shared by millions outside Russia when accounts of the mass murder spread throughout the civilized world, bringing resentment on purely humanitarian grounds. Many felt close to the Romanovs because the much-photographed grand duchesses had set the pace for fashion designs, or because they had suffered through the illnesses of the sickly Czarevich, or because they had been moved by accounts of the Romanov's steadily worsening living conditions as prisoners at Tobolsk and Ekaterinburg. Some of these foreigners were promptly hooked by the odd magic of the Romanov Mystique. It perseveres to this day in many parts of the world.

Others are quite immune to any such sentimental appeal. Viewing the passing of czarism as a long-overdue token of the crackup of Europe's absurd caste systems, they find in Nicholas's countenance only the archetype of that decorative and relatively useless individual, the Edwardian Age patrician; the kind of face seen in the early years of the century in the club windows of London and New York, in boxes at the opera, at Derby, in the grand hotels of Europe's spas and at Longchamps during the high fashion season.

The cause of all these varied effects on others was dichotomous. Nicholas was two czars at the same time. One was real; the other was a glamorized version. The real one was short, a bit gnomelike, but not unattractive. The glamorized version was raised several inches in height and otherwise beautified by chamberlains, cameramen, photographic experts and publishers for the special benefit of a more distant public and the readers of newspapers, magazines and books.

The real czar was a bantam in the royal arena of European rulers. He was a diminutive and unprepossessing figure with very short legs, an outsize head and torso. His ears were large. On the top of his head the parietal bones of the skull rose to an almost abnormal height. The retouchers erased this feature. They also reduced the size of the ears. Nicholas was the smallest of his over-six-foot father's sons. The best documentation of his adult years places his height as between five-seven and five-seven-and-a-half, but there are those who saw a great deal of him who vow that his true stature was just a shade over five feet four. If so, then three inches plus were part of the visual mythology.

He was anything but a commanding presence at a military review dominated by big Cossacks and husky members of the Guards Regiments. He was particularly unimpressive on horseback where some detractors equated his appearance with that of a light little jockey bedecked in a general's racing colors. His short legs seemed barely able to reach the stirrups. Accordingly, the court photographers distributed few prints which showed lateral views of their mounted monarch. They also saw to it, wherever possible, that no group pictures were sent out in which Nicholas's figure was over-whelmed by the presence of those much taller. This became pro-gressively a testier problem after the start of World War I with photographs that called for the joint posing of Nicholas and the Commander-in-Chief of the Russian Armies in the field, the Grand Duke Nicholas Nicolaievich, the skyscraping soldier of six feet six.

It took World War I to scrape most of the romantic patina from Nicholas. Then Russia's appalling manpower losses (total casual-ties were 9.15 millions) led the list of the twelve Allies, and her acute shortages of food, ammunition and materiel spread gloom throughout the nation and tended to depict Nicholas and all his works as embodiments of failure. What prestige he had gained plummeted in the world, even among monarchists. Other crowned heads were forced to realize that any close identification with him could cost them their own thrones. Nicholas acquired a harrowed look. Pictures taken of him near the fighting front are those of a starkly worried man with deep shadows under his eyes. By 1917 the real Nicholas and the imagemakers' creation were allowed to merge. The time for make-believe was over.

Nicholas II was more of a Jonah figure than an imperial one when the Allies saw that they might have to do something about rescuing him. It was clear that the rescue, if there were to be one, would have to be muted. In the first place, Nicholas's life would be endangered the minute it became known that he was being moved out of Russia. The anti-Czarists would be enraged. They were planning a spectacular trial in which "Citizen Romanov" would be prosecuted for his "crimes against humanity." Second, any foreign government whose aid to him became known could be subject to violent criticism from its own citizenry for trying to perpetuate the influence of the kind of absolute monarch that history had rejected. The ensuing wave of public outrage, conceivably, could sweep such a government out of office.

To Nicholas's rescuers fell the problem of dealing with a man who virtually guaranteed perils to any group that was found help-ing him — a man who was almost as much of a failure in his own opinion as he was in the eyes of the world. The challenge was not inspiring. There was no place in the world where cheers awaited him. If there would come a time when his once-imperial presence would provide hope to some new order, say to Russia reconquered by the Whites, it was a long way off.

The problem was further complicated by the great number of lower-level rescue plans being cooked up by Czarist cliques of all sorts. Anywhere along the line the amateurs could stumble all over the professionals. The effort could become a slapstick comedy. There was also evidence that the Germans themselves, for political reasons, mostly to make the Treaty of Brest-Litovsk seem more palatable to the Russian people, wanted to use Nicholas's prestige, or what was left of it, as a rallying force for all anti-Bolsheviks everywhere. They plotted to bring the Romanovs to Germany, with or without their consent. An actual kidnapping was considered. One of the pro-Romanov organizations which was formed at the time, for example, was the League for the Restoration of the Russian Empire. It had agents in several foreign capitals.

An interesting document that relates to the League was found recently in the Public Record Office in London. It is a decoded message to Lord Hardinge, in the Foreign Office, from Sir H. Humbold, British Minister in Berne. Classified as "secret," it arrived in London at 10:30 p.m., July 21, 1918, four days after the Romanovs were "assassinated." Here is the text:

"I am forwarding by safe opportunity a letter addressed to Mr. Balfour by section of League for restoration of Russian Empire which has reached me through agent of this Legation in Geneva who received it in turn from Messrs. Svatkovsky and Poznansky whose names are known to you. The letter is sealed, and similar communications are stated to have been addressed to Italian and French Prime Ministers.

"I understand that contents of the letter are as follows:

"Grand Duke Leuchtenberg has recently been at Berlin in conjunction [sic] with position of the ex-Tsar to whom Germans have offered assistance which His Majesty has declined. Berlin Government have now approached the above-mentioned Swiss section of the League as to whether they agree to plot hatched by Germany for kidnapping the ex-Tsar and bringing him to Germany with or without his consent. In their communication to you the League ask to be furnished with views of Entente on this scheme . . . Svatkovsky hopes for an affirmative reply while Poznansky hopes there will be no reply at all from the Allies consulted.

"Poznansky, who secretly informed British agent of contents of the letter, also stated that the question of kidnapping the ex-Tsar to Germany had no interest for League, whose hopes for restoration are centered on the Tsarevitch.

"He argues that if scheme succeeds League will be bound hand and feet to Germany, while if it fails odium will recoil on League. Consequently he hopes for negative reply from Entente which will divest the League of responsibility and enable them to return evasive reply. Svatkovsky on the other hand hopes that plan will succeed.

"Repeated to Paris and Rome."

It is now apparent that the Germans, Japanese, British, Americans and Russians of both Red and White persuasions all took part in saving the lives of the Romanovs. If the manner in which they did so seems unnecessarily devious in the nineteen-seventies, one must be forgiving enough to recall the upheaving effects that World War I exerted on the world's statesmen, and the fact that of all periods of the war, 1918 brought more quick changes of outlook, month by month, than any other year.

In January the Germans seemed on the verge of victory and were still a formidable military threat to Bolshevik Russia. In August they seemed to be nearing the verge of defeat. By November the Allies had won; the Germans were crushed, and the Kaiser had fled to Holland. The Berlin Government was no longer a mortal concern to anyone. But by that same month — November — the menace of Bolshevism had become an internal threat to all the losers and to some of the winners. Harassed also by the scourge of famine and a worldwide epidemic of influenza which, by 1919, had killed an estimated twenty million persons, the year 1918 was one to boggle the mind. It was a year in which those who planned the Romanovs' rescue in the spring and summer could not have come close to foreseeing what the later months would bring.

Why were so many nations willing to aid in the covert rescue of someone as relatively spurned and powerless as ex-Czar Nicholas II?

By way of an answer, there are good conjectures that come to mind more than half a century after the fact. At least four members of the Allied coalition shared a common obligation of honor to a Russian monarch who had unhesitatingly committed his armies to offensives against the Germans on one front, and against the Austro-Hungarians on another, in the early weeks of the war. Those campaigns cost the lives of more than a quarter of a million Russians. Nevertheless, they diverted enough of the Kaiser's divisions from the West to save France from collapse. The Allies who most benefited from the Russian sacrifice were France, Britain, Italy, Japan and, more latterly, the United States. Four of the five had additional special reasons to help Nicholas.

For the British, he was their own king's first cousin. For the French, he was an ardent disciple of the Franco-Russian Alliance which was cemented by his father, Czar Alexander III, in 1894 — the year Alexander died and Nicholas succeeded him — and which almost overnight rendered the specter of German militarism far less unbearable to the Quai d'Orsay.

For the Japanese, their own Imperial Family owed the Romanovs a debt of honor incurred in 1891. That was the year in which Nicholas, then Czarevich on a tour of the Far East, was assaulted and nearly killed in Otsu by a saber-swinging member of his Japanese guard. Emperor Mutsuhito regarded the incident as a national disgrace to be expunged whenever a chance came.

For the Americans, President Wilson's "Fourteen Points" formula for settling the peace of Europe was also aimed at inducing the Reds and Whites of Russia to resolve their differences along with all the other combatants. Having a "Czar in the cellar," ready to reappear at a psychological moment, could have had, from Wilson's viewpoint, a beneficial effect on his efforts to resolve the Russian question in the same thrust in which he was determined to solve the European question at the peace conferences, especially when Nicholas had sponsored both international conventions at the Hague (1899 and 1907) from which had come the International

Court of Justice. Protocols of the latter were not far removed from Wilson's dream of the League of Nations.

For the Germans there was another set of reasons. In the first place, the Kaiser was related in different ways to both Nicholas and Alexandra. Since the German Emperor was in a position to dictate terms to the Bolsheviks at the Treaty of Brest-Litovsk, it is not surprising that the Reds agreed in a secret codicil of that treaty to grant safe passage to the Imperial Family of Russia. Second, the Wilhelmstrasse felt it needed Nicholas's public support to make the Brest-Litovsk Treaty more digestible to the Russian people and thus enable more German troops to be freed for the Western Front. (Unable to get Nicholas's personal endorsement of the treaty, the Kaiser's Government actually sent agents as far as the Crimea to try to persuade various Romanov relatives, including grand dukes, to make statements in support of the treaty. They failed to do so.) Third, the Bolsheviks in Western Europe were fast becoming the Red Menace that threatened to overthrow other monarchies, the Kaiser's included. The resurrection of Nicholas could help rally Whites, the Germans thought, against the Reds. We know now — as already shown — that the Germans were so anxious to lure Nicholas into their custody by offering asylum from the Kaiser in 1918, that when he first declined the invitation, a plot was actually hatched in Germany to kidnap the Romanovs and import them against their will.

For the Bolshevik leaders in the Kremlin, the motive to help the Romanovs was purely a matter of their own survival. They knew they would risk a resumption of the German offensive, a crushing defeat and the end of their own regime, if they failed to live up to the stipulations at Brest-Litovsk.

Finally, whether German or anti-German, Red or anti-Red, all the nations involved in the Romanov liberation were pragmatic enough to realize that secrecy was paramount. They knew that if the highly anti-Czarist district soviets in western Siberia ever got wind of the rescue plot, the Romanovs, way out in the Siberian city of Tobolsk, would be rounded up and shot no matter what Lenin or Sverdlov decreed. None knew it better than Lenin and Sverdlov — unless, perhaps, it was Sokolnikov. He was the Bolsheviks' senior

H.M.S. *Calypso* was one of the busiest members of the rescue fleet which the Admiralty sent to the Black Sea in the 1918–1919 period. Hubert M. Limbrick served as its "captain's messenger." *Calypso* had a 344-man crew, was 450 feet long, made 30 knots and was armed with five six-inch guns and eight torpedo tubes. *(Photo by British Admiralty)*

Hubert M. Limbrick as a 16-year-old messenger for Captain Thesiger, skipper of *Calypso;* and as he looks today (his face bears scars from Bolshevik gunfire). Limbrick is sure that Anastasia stayed in Capt. Thesiger's cabin.

Peter Bessell, former member of the House of Commons, who was largely instrumental in digging the Chivers Papers out of their hiding place in Washington, D. C. *(Fabian Bachrach)*

Jeremy Thorpe, Leader of the Liberal Party, is a frequent visitor to the U.S. where he attended school during World War II. Shown here during one of his campaigns.

Sergius Riis *(above, left)* in full dress Naval uniform, shortly after World War I, and *(above)* as he looked in his late fifties, on the eve of Pearl Harbor. Sergius's son, Earl *(left)*, born in Warsaw, Poland, at home in Plantation, Florida with his wife and their children.

(Opposite) Vice Admiral Newton A. McCully, boss, friend and chief sponsor of his two talented Naval Intelligence "spooks," Sergius M. Riis and Hugo Wm. Koehler. All three were highly decorated for their services in Russia. *(U.S. Navy photograph)*

Hugo Koehler *(extreme left)*, puffing away on a pipe, with three other admiral's aides, and *(below)* in a casual pose with a young friend, March 20, 1921. Koehler could also be brusque and stiff *(below, left)* when the mood struck him. (Warsaw, Nov. 11, 1921, as U.S. Naval Attaché.) For his outstanding accomplishments, Koehler was awarded the Navy Cross and several Czarist decorations. *(At bottom)* Koehler takes what his album calls "A quiet stroll in Cracow," on April 18, 1922.

Rear Admiral Spencer S. Wood introduced Hugo Koehler to his daughter, Margaretta ("Maggie") in Washington. There began the friendship of a lifetime. She was as versatile as he, including amateur acting.

This is how the elusive Chicago lawyer, Roy C. Woods, looked more than fifty-one years ago when American novelist Kenneth Roberts reported that Woods — working out of Warsaw — was secretly dickering with the Czar's daughter, Tatiana, in the hope of bringing her to America in 1923. Mr. Woods, still alive at 95, would only say that he was on a confidential mission for Secretary of State Charles Evans Hughes. *(Robert Saborski)*

Claiborne Pell, U.S. Senator from Rhode Island, has spent years trying to assemble the facts about the Naval Intelligence feats of his stepfather, Commander Hugo William Koehler.

The striking resemblance of the two imperial cousins, Czar Nicholas II *(left)* and the Prince of Wales, later King George V, at Cowes, summer of 1909. *(U.P.I. photo)*

(*Left*) About five months before their wedding, the Czarevich Nicholas and his fiancée, Princess Alix of Hesse, made a visit to England in 1894. Picture taken during that visit. (*Below*) Each of the Czar's five children signed this photograph, taken in 1913, a year before World War I. Left to right, Marie, Tatiana, Anastasia, Olga and Alexei.

(Right) Colonel Michal Goleniewski in 1964, New York City. *(Below)* A grave bearing the name of "Michal Goleniewski," in the parish cemetery, Wolsztyn, Poland. Colonel Goleniewski claims it is the grave of Nicholas II, deceased in 1952. *(both photos: Robert Speller & Sons)*

Robert Wilton, correspondent of *The Times* of London, who was sent to Russia to assist in research on the Romanov's disappearance. His copies of the Sokolov Investigation papers are in the Houghton Library of Harvard University.

Major Joseph Lasies, a French official who helped to gather information about the Romanovs' disappearance. His conclusion was that they all escaped.

Mrs. Eugenia Smith claims to be the Czar's daughter, Anastasia. She wrote an autobiography which states that she escaped the "assassination" and came to Illinois in the 1920s. *(LIFE magazine)*

"The Woman in Warsaw," who many insiders believe is the Czar's daughter, Marie. She has told friends that she is the mother of Colonel Goleniewski. *(Robert Speller & Sons)*

Lord Hardinge of Penshurst, Permanent Under Secretary for Foreign Affairs, former Viceroy of India, and close friend of Edward VII and George V. (*Times History of The War*)

(*Below*) Lt. Col. Sir William Wiseman, Bart., C.B., when of the British Intelligence Service in the United States, 1917–1918. (*New York Public Library*)

General Jozef Pilsudski, hero of modern Poland. In 1914 *(above)* as organizer of The Polish Legion; and *(right)* in 1935, the year of his death. *(Pilsudski Institute of America)*

It was during the reign of the Emperor Mutsuhito *(above)*, more commonly known as "Méiji," that the Imperial Japanese family incurred what they later considered a debt of honor to the Romanovs. During the reign of his son, Emperor Yoshihito *(right)*, they discharged this debt by helping to rescue the Romanovs. *(U.P.I. photos)*

representative at the final signing of the Brest-Litovsk Treaty on March 3, 1918.

Thus secrecy was essential everywhere for the short range. But secrecy for the longer range was required particularly in France (French Army officials helped the Romanovs pass through Odessa safely by politely looking the other way), and in Britain. Revelations of secret government involvement in the rescue by either of those two nations could easily have given their own local communists and left-wingers a potent political weapon. (This is doubtless why the Americans took over the rescue's riskiest part.) So, long after the Romanovs had reached neutral territory, there was virtually no one who knew about their escape who could see any advantage in making it public. The only incentive might come from signs that the Whites were going to win the Red-White war. This went on and on for more than two years after World War I was over. The signs never came. When the Whites conclusively lost, late in 1920, that settled it. Unveiling the story thereafter, it was thought, offered more liabilities than assets to all concerned. For more than half a century that has remained the verdict on this state secret of World War I.

CHAPTER 7

THE CHIVERS DISPATCHES

When I first received my set of copies of the Chivers messages I signed an agreement, at Peter Bessell's request, that I would not release them before the White House gave us the go-ahead. I am now disclosing their contents more than two years afterwards because (1) in 1973 I received a two-and-a-half month advance notice that the firm release date would be March 31 of that year and I regarded that notice as irreversible; (2) the Chivers Papers were not legally classified at the time the copies were given to me by Mr. Bessell; (3) there is nothing in them which, by the widest stretch of imagination, could endanger the security of any nation in 1975, and, (4) the time is long overdue for scholars and historians to make their own evaluation of the papers. They should note that the Chivers Papers, Lord Hardinge's Letter and the Bulgarian Version of what happened in 1918 and 1919 interlock in time and place and couple together like three cars of a train going from three adjacent localities to a common destination.

Are these documents and versions totally accurate?

There again the reader should try to determine his own answer. I can offer three suggestions:

To the best of my knowledge and belief they tell a story which is substantially true and substantially new.

I believe they give an account of the rescue of the last Imperial Family of Russia which exposes as a complete fraud the widely accepted news of the Romanovs' "assassination."

I have no doubt that there are a few diversionary entries and "red herrings" in one or two of the Chivers messages. The security problems of the rescue party were grave. Since its changing itinerary was being sent from time to time by wireless, in code, some precautions might have been taken against possible interception by hostile elements who could decode the messages. Most codes in those days were much simpler than they are now. I have indicated where and in what messages such diversions might have been planted — but I'm not sure they were.

The Chivers Papers are published in this chapter in the chronological order in which President Wilson must have read them, and in the exact form that I received them from Peter Bessell. The abbreviations for names of the members of the Imperial Family used in the papers are as follows:

His M: Nicholas II, Czar of Russia.

Her M: Alexandra Feodorovna, Empress of Russia.

G. Duke or Grand D: Alexei, Czarevich of Russia (the youngest child and only son of Nicholas and Alexandra).

G. Duchess or Grand D: Olga, Tatiana, Marie and Anastasia, daughters of Nicholas and Alexandra.

G.D.s: Refers to all four daughters.

JULY 10, 1918

The plan is now in readiness. Today I visited the chief of the staff whose excellent English made my understanding of him simple. He is the equal of a Colonel in the Imperial Japanese Army his name being Kiyaki.

A member of his personal entourage skilled in the arts of defense will accompany the driver who was formerly a member of His M's personal staff at Tsarkoe and who will have with him two loyal Russians skilled in the use of firearms and able should [need] arise to repair the engine.

His M and family will be aroused at about the hour of 2 AM and will be escorted to the truck which has been well tested by the engineer and will be waiting outside the servants' door.

The journey will be along good roads to the house 15 miles nor' nor'-west where resides the trade minister. It is a safe place of refuge surrounded by walls and gardens with but two gateways each with a guard house. There are three floors and cellars and ample clean water from two wells within the gardens. There is no electrical lighting but this matters little as where there are supplies these failed long ago.

No member of the retinue will go with His M and his family, and two have volunteered for the camouflage plan. His M is much disturbed for them and greatly moved by such devoted service.

His M is telling nothing to Her M or the G.D.s or the Grand D. He thinks it best for them not to be informed for fear an idle word may betray the plan. They will be told when he arouses them.

The journey will last about one hour or perhaps a little longer. The road will be clear and guards posted. The curfew does not end til 6 AM.

Several crucial items of intelligence are yielded in this first dispatch. One is that the Japanese are handling the getaway and early sequestration. Another is that Kiyaki is "the equal of" a Japanese army colonel. That would appear to indicate that he was an agent of the Japanese secret service and not, at least at the time, in the army. A third is that two members of "the retinue" have "volunteered for the camouflage plan" which, we are soon to learn, is the real murder of two persons which the rescuers want to have construed as the assassination of the Romanovs. These two are never identified. Finally, the expression "nor' nor'-west" hints that a naval agent wrote the message.

JULY 18, 1918

The plan worked thus. At the hour of 2 the guard aroused His M and His M aroused Her M and each G. Duchess. The G. Duke was carried from the bed by His M to the stair head where they all walked to the ground floor to meet the waiting guard.

The personal retinue was not disturbed because His M did not want them to know the plan which grieved him in this particular. Tea and broth with bread were served up to His M and his family in the passageway to the door in the back. They stood while eating and did not speak.

At the hour of 3 the guard took up his place outside the door in the back now unlatched and opened.

In the lane the truck in readiness with the chosen driver.

It was a sultry night. Few stars or moonlight. First to leave were Her M and the youngest G.D. Then the G.D.s Olga and Marie. Then the G.D. Tatiana and the G. Duke. Then last came His M who thanked the guard.

The engine started on two turns and the truck was away turning to the right and there its journey started.

The guard began his wretched task within the house and in the large room chosen for it. By half past the hour of 4 all was done and the two corpses taken to the [second] truck which was driven up to the door a little time before. It started up at the first turn and was away. By this hour it is day and all would have [been] seen but for the curfew.

His M will not be known without his whiskers and with his hair so long. Her M refused to change her styles but is so changed (physically) I doubt her sister would acknowledge her. The G.D.s were most compliant and snipped off each others hair. The Grand D. has no disguise and we feared he must be detected but Her M said people knew him best in Naval dress. This did not allay my worry for he wore uniforms but rarely here.

Here begins the disguise of the cleanshaven but long-haired patriarch that was to serve Nicholas in such good stead for his future years undercover. This message also makes it clear that the two "volunteers" were, indeed, via the guard's "wretched task," transformed into "two corpses." Still no clue to their identity is given. There were four members of Nicholas's personal entourage in Ipatiev House on July 16, 1918. They were Dr. Eugene Botkin, the physician; Anna Demidova, Alexandra's maidservant; Kharitonov, the cook, and Trupp, a manservant.

It is anyone's guess as to which two were murdered. From the rescuers' standpoint, it seems probable that they would have wished to retain the services of Dr. Botkin and perhaps those of Alexandra's maid, Anna Demidova. That would have left the two manservants, Trupp and Kharitonov, as the best candidates for the "camouflage plan." Did they in truth volunteer or were they chosen? Nicholas is described as "grieved" about all this, but his grief seems to have vanished quickly. A third message, describing his arrival at the Japanese hideout, pictures him in "high good spirits." That was less than an hour after leaving Ipatiev House.

JULY 19, 1918

It is with consuming pride I now complete my report to you of even date. His M and his family made good the journey in under the hour the engine not failing or giving need for attention all along the way. It was day and brightly sunny with the journey over when they got to the destination. Having not stopped upon the road Her M was much fatigued and was carried indoors, the others entering on foot. His M in high good spirits called out his greeting cordially to his new guardians and was taken with no delay to the chief of the staff who handed credentials to His M to see. His M was pleased with these, and the G.D.s Marie and Tatiana inspected the quarters testing in all places the locks and devices for their safety. He was well pleased. His M will have the biggest room and Her M the next. The G.D.s O and T will share another and the G.D.s M and A yet a fourth. The G.D. will have a room below with his guard to share it.

Breakfast was served up at about half past 5 AM and quickly eaten then His M and the family retired for sleep.

No word has come from the Provisional Government at Moscow that I have heard about. Back at the town word was read to the people in a public place and well taken by them.

The plan has thus proved satisfactory and pleasing to all.

Three points in this message are worth noting. One is that Nicholas was so "pleased" with the credentials shown him by Kiyaki because, perhaps, they included a personal message from Emperor Yoshihito. Another is the reference to "the Provisional Government," a phrase used to apply to the Bolshevik Regime by the agent in several more dispatches before he switched to the more accurate designation, the Soviet Government.

Another is the mention of the truck engine "not failing." Considering that both the first and second trucks used on that fateful morning at Ipatiev House started almost the moment that their motors were turned over, and that trucks and cars carried the rescue party months later over 1800 miles of Russia's primitive roads, the part played in the whole saga by the fledgling motor vehicle industry was not inconsiderable. The story is worth a book in itself when all the makes and models are traced down. It was, for example, an American Ford car fan, Dr. Armand Hammer of New York, who three years after this episode persuaded Lenin, Trotsky and Henry Ford to give him sole rights to sell the Fordson tractor in Bolshevik Russia.

In agonizing days awaiting the chance to leave the Japanese mission near Ekaterinburg, all kinds of worries came to the fretful Romanovs. The American agent wirelessed a request to Washington for more money. He got less than half of the $200,000 he asked for.

Nicholas grew perturbed over the British refusal to send funds. Alexandra became so fearful of catching the flu that she gargled throughout the days with a mixture of thymol and permanganate. For a while she staved off the affliction which hit most of the others. She busied herself with her crochet needles making cotton and silk lace wristlets for her daughters' frocks.

Nicholas decided to perk up his German in practice conversations with a guard named Svenski. This could be interpreted as a sign that he had begun to adjust his mind to the idea of accepting refuge in Germany.

The start of the following dispatch of August 24th leads one to imagine there is a message missing from the file. The phrase "in the matter of my wireless of today" smacks of being a reference to which further explanation is being made. A full reading of the message dissipates that idea. All points seem to be covered in it; especially the need for bribery of all factions on a grand scale.

AUGUST 24, 1918

In the matter of my wireless of today the sum required for a safe journey through the territory to the Southern shores is large. Payment will be made to guards supplied by the Provisional Government in Moscow who risk their lives as do all taking part. And payment will be made to local provisional governments in control of territories His M and family will traverse. Then there will be payment to other local army groups or armies in territory they control and who are not friendly to the Provisional Government in Moscow. You will surely know the territory is captured and lost and then regained from time to time and often the Provisional Government in Moscow is not in control and it follows payment must be made to those who are.

His Imperial Majesty of Japan has supplied money about the equal of $75,000 but this is short and no less than 200,000 dollars will be enough. As the plan is to pass responsibility to England when the Southern shores are reached, when all will then be simple, will not England pay a share in the cost of the perilous first journey and you the rest?

The coded name of Chivers has been chosen but no reason for such name made known to me.

I have no more instruction on the route because I think the chief of the staff has not agreed with the Russian who may not yet have been instructed by his Provisional Government in Moscow.

The chief of staff is not given to much communication but I think him not unfriendly in his oriental manner. He is exceedingly respectful to His M and his family and takes trouble to provide such comforts as he can.

The poor Romanovs! The leader of every faction wanted a payoff. Not one seemed willing to serve for nothing. Faced with demands of that sort, it is easy to see why our man in Siberia asked for $200,000. It is interesting that Japan thought enough of the operation to contribute $75,000, and Woodrow Wilson matched it in the reply.

Here, too, emerges the code name "Chivers." If it originated in London it might have been in honor of a famous brand of English marmalade, with a bit of mutedly humorous tribute to a very "sticky" situation. If it originated in Washington it might have been thought up by the sly and well-read Colonel House in a deferential nod to an obscure American poet, Thomas H. Chivers of Georgia. (House was a Texan.) Chivers was one of seven children. His poetry is preoccupied with the theme of life after death. Both could be remote allusions to the seven Romanovs which few, with the exception of Virginia-born Woodrow Wilson, would have understood.

SEPTEMBER 1, 1918 (*Not Verbatim*)*
Reverse message from Washington

Which states that the request contained in the last cable has been considered by "W. W. and his private cabinet Secretary" and we do not think that it will be possible to get any cash out of the English because their attitude is one of [verbatim] unwilling assistance [end verbatim] but that the Ambassador will be asked to make a request to his Government.

Meanwhile W. W. has agreed to send an amount equal to that provided by the Japanese Emperor and it will be in gold rubles.

Then come strange sentence [verbatim] His Imperial Majesty would have been more provident had he made available some part of his resources in England for such a purpose as this [end verbatim].

In future years, we may hear a lot more of this reference to the ex-Czar's "resources in England." It has been widely reported that Nicholas deposited large sums in England, France and the United States before and during the early months of World War I. These funds, according to credible sources, were quite distinct from those placed in foreign banks by the Czarist government and later claimed, with partial success, by the Soviets.

There is no public record of Nicholas's personal funds ever having been disbursed to his heirs. If such funds do, in fact, exist, some lively litigation over them can now be expected from Romanov survivors and other claimants.

SEPTEMBER 6, 1918

His M's in good heart and spirits. Less so is Her M. She dreads the epidemic for herself and gargles many times a day with a compound of thymol and permanganate. His M sleeps well and eats

---

*As explained in an earlier chapter, Mr. Bessell had to condense some of the messages.

all that is put upon his table. His face is lined and his complexion pallid but his eyes are clear and he bears himself alert and high. He speaks little of affairs of State and occupies his mind with hopes of a peaceful future for himself and family. He likes conversing in the German language and a Guard named Svenski gives him lessons to improve him in it. He reads all English books and shows no regard for the library of Russian volumes here. Now and then he reads aloud to the G.D. Marie first in English and then he translates the passage into the German tongue. His M and the G.D. are reading Dickens' "Copperfield" in this fashion.

Her M uses the crochet hook and is making laces from silk and cotton threads. It is reported to me Her M explained to the G.D. Marie that she is making wristlets for frocks for the G.D. and her sisters. She sighs for breath and holds her left hand to her throat. She eats thus. When meals are served up she watches while her family eats. His M coaxes her to no avail. Then when they are done she eats the now cold fare leaving most. All the while His M and the G.D.s Marie and Tatiana wait for her to finish. The other girls ask to be excused and are so allowed to leave the table.

SEPTEMBER 14, 1918

Daily it is more difficult to be sure these wireless codes are sent to you. The chief of the staff is most correct and careful and doesn't dispatch papers unless he is sure they complete their journey. But the territory around us is changing hands and if towns are governed by a soviet loyal to the government at Moscow it doesn't mean that even the nearest village is loyal also. Journeys are filled with these hazards and at all times it is my fear the wirelesses will be captured before they can be sent. So do not ask for more please. I send all I can.

It was good the Spanish flu did not come to these parts until [the] week last gone as food and medicines were scarce and had His M and his family been weak and hungry the illness would have been severe.

His M had but a touch and is well recovered from it. Her M has been most fortunate and seems to have avoided the complaint. The oldest two G.D.s likewise. The G.D. M and the G.D. A have been very poorly with high fevers which are now abated. The G.D. was not so ill but is listless and still stops in bed all day. He is of moody disposition and demands at all times to be treated as a prince when he is then more friendly.

It is difficult to try to tell you when they will leave for the journey. The chief of the staff gets reports of conditions in each place but these are often many days old and not dependable. He fears most we will be encircled by unfriendly Russians who may recognize his charges. That this has not thus far happened here is a god-sent miracle. It was still the plan to leave this month but between the sickness and the fighting I don't expect to see them go for many days or weeks.

SEPTEMBER 22, 1918 — *(Not Verbatim)*

For three days before this date three "American Agents" visited the house and stayed in the servants quarters. They tried to over-hear the private conversations of the Emperor and Empress but since the agents spoke English and Russian, but not German, they were somewhat put out when, after the first night, the couple talked in German. These are examples of the terminology: "these persons concealed themselves most cunningly as suggested by the chief of the staff who had made ready for them" and "on the second night of their vigil His M and Her M conversed in the German tongue and naught was understood" and "this night they left with little of much merit to their credit."

What they did hear was the couple discussing the Empress' dis-satisfaction with food, heating arrangements, etc., her conviction that her heart was "too fragile" for the journey, that her pillow was too hard and too large and the Emperor "exploring each of her complaints most sympathetically with no traces of impatience." Also the Emperor doubting the ability of the Americans to work out any plan and route for the next part of the journey because he regarded them as an undisciplined lot containing elements of Russian Jewish refugees who, he thought, would bump them off given the slightest opportunity. He said he hoped that the Japs would continue to be responsible with the Americans playing only a secondary role. He also grumbled about the British not having communicated with him.

Most significant of all is that the Emperor expressed several times his firm belief that ultimately they would be rescued by the Kaiser who he referred to as "our cousin Wilhelm" and once as "William." There seemed to be nothing but friendliness in his attitude towards him.

SEPTEMBER 29, 1918
Reverse Message

As conveyed to you on September 22, His Britannic Majesty's Government through the Principal Secretary of State has informed us that [it] is not able to furnish any help beyond that which it has already agreed to provide.

I am now instructed to inform you that the money dispatched to you through our accredited representative in Archangel is all that can be provided.

OCTOBER 9, 1918

Much concern was caused by your wireless saying the British will not pay any sum and you will not supply more. If the plan and mission fail now the fault for this will not be mine or the chief of the staff. Our best that we shall do may be unavailing and longer time, with attendant risks, will now be consumed to make safe the plan.

OCTOBER 23, 1918

His M called for me the day before yesterday seemingly because Her M is much disturbed and disquieted by prolongation of their [think word was "sojurn"] at this place. I placated His M as much as I was able and told my belief we shall soon be away. Then I asked him much about the revolution which he said was caused to his mind by the dissatisfaction of the Hebrew peoples in his Country and without his borders. To this cause His M attributes most that has occurred and told that he thinks the Hebrew peoples gave of their bounty to cause the revolution which he told me the people of his Country do not want save for a few discontented souls. Until this dreadful war he told me his peoples were all well cared for and loved him greatly and his father and grandfather likewise. Always he told me it was the Hebrew peoples who stirred the pot.

To my great surprise His M asked me of the Treaty in which he is not versed. I was discrete [*sic.*] and told only a little of what I know of the disputations between Mister Leon Trotsky and Mister Lenin and how the disputations were concerned with the safety of his person.

He was eager to learn of this and how H.I.M. the Kaiser had required of his defeated foes that they be sure of His M safe passage to a country of exile. I told then of the part which is a condition that this safety be assured and that it could not be printed and public. To this he said he understood and was satisfied.

His M is now almost like he was before '14 at times most gay and playful with his daughters who are most affectionate to him. Such teases are the younger G.D.s that we sometimes think they are not as careful of their safety as one would wish them to be.

Her M is not of any higher spirits and eats late and sits looking from the window to the west where the summer garden is no longer so beautiful which is good because it is peaceful now and the village people might at another time of year wish to visit this garden as they did in summers past.

Her M uses still her hook and now is making laces for her frocks this comforts her. Her M is not of domestic turn of mind and seems not to care to ask the servants of their menu plans so the G.D. O does this and although there is little change of fare plans for varied dishes.

A day has passed and now I can tell of more. His M is easy with me and called upon me today to tell of the Treaty. We talked for an hour or perhaps more in his own bedroom and I was bound to tell him of H.I.M. the Kaiser's offer of refuge which seemed not displeasing to him. Of how Mr. T. had disowned a plan for his M's safety and took no more participation.

The Chief of the staff has now a plan and when I told His M he broke from our discussion to hasten to Her M and did not resume with me.

Here is the first reference to the secret codicil in the Treaty of Brest-Litovsk — the one in which the Germans stipulated a "safe passage" for the Romanovs — which more than helf a century later was discovered by Peter Bessell through confidential sources in London.

It is also interesting to note that by October, 1918 the Kaiser was secretly urging Nicholas to come to Germany. Nicholas had wanted asylum for his family in England. Months before he had spurned the thought of accepting refuge from the hated Germans. But after the British had turned him down it is notable — as per this October message — that the renewed invitation from the Kaiser "seemed not displeasing to him."

Here also we get a very strong hint that the safe passage for the Romanovs might have been a bone of contention between Lenin and Trotsky; why Trotsky walked out of the first sessions of Brest-Litovsk; why Lenin sent a replacement (Sokolnikov) to sign the treaty which contained the secret codicil.

Trotsky makes no mention of the codicil in his memoirs and, in fact, writes only a hearsay account of the Romanovs' "assassination." It is not by any means impossible that Trotsky was never told the truth about the codicil by Lenin, Sverdlov, Sokolnikov or any of the few high Bolshevik leaders who knew about it. After Brest-Litovsk, Trotsky was shifted from his foreign affairs post to take charge of the Red Army. He was at the front when Nicholas's "execution" was announced in July. A. H. Bruce Lockhart, in his book, *British Agent,* reports that Trotsky was so miffed at the terms of the Treaty of Brest-Litovsk that he refused to attend the ratification ceremonies held in Moscow on March 10, 1918.

At first Nicholas was buoyed by the feeling that the war was nearing an end. It seems that he guessed wrong, however, about the victor. The news of the armistice and the Central Powers' defeat plunged him into gloom. The night he heard about it he became so morose that he couldn't eat his supper.

But the tidings had exactly the opposite effect on Alexandra, his German-born wife — the figure whom many gossips in old St. Petersburg charged with spying for the Wilhelmstrasse. (A Hessian princess, she was also the granddaughter of Queen Victoria.) She is reported as being absolutely elated over word that the Kaiser had fled into exile.

Historians may be surprised by this message. They might have expected quite contrary reactions — Alexandra to be despondent over the final defeat of her native land and the loss of its sovereign; Nicholas to be cheered by the demise of Russia's former enemy. But partial explanations of Nicholas's gloom could be (a) that the armistice blasted all hope of finding refuge in Germany under the Kaiser's protection, and (b) that the armistice terms offered no possibility for a reprieve for all that czarism stood for. In other words, it was another defeat for his regime; another crown in the dust.

At last, in the setting of the snow-covered Urals, the plans are set for their long trek to Odessa. Alexandra became obsessed by the challenge of its hazards.

NOVEMBER 3, 1918 *(Not Verbatim)*

They seem to have had a great deal of news about the progress of the war and this seems to have pleased them. The Emperor believes that it will soon be over and that there will be peace. Interesting to note that he does not make any mention of his attitude towards Russia. It is reported that he now feels happy about his

German lessons and that he is working very hard on them with the Guard, whose name is not mentioned this time. It seems that the Grand Duchess Anastasia is not being very helpful about learning the language but that the Emperor is still working hard with Marie on it and she is responding well. The other two [no mention of Alexei] girls are making good progress. The Empress does not do any more needle work and spends most of her time in bed and the Emperor is very patient with her. Although a doctor who seems to be visiting her pretty often he does not think there is much the matter with her.

Long message because the night before it was written there was fear of some sort of attack on the nearby town [not named] by a "marauding group of soldiers not loyal to the Soviet at Moscow" goes on about whether family should have been alerted but as they were not they did not hear about it all until the following day. First hint of any criticism of the chief of staff.

NOVEMBER 12, 1918 *(Not Verbatim)*

Although it had been expected for some days the news of the armistice did not reach them until the date of this dispatch which must have been written late in the evening. The Emperor "was much depressed withdrawing into himself and staying alone for some hours." This was attributed to the end of the war not resulting in the expected victory for the Imperial Russia but instead a defeat for the Central Powers and a defeat for all that he had tried to build in Russia. He told his family that now the war was over he did not think it likely that the Allies would interest themselves further in the fate of Russia and referred to the Democracies as being drained by the war and likely to become socialist States also. The Empress on the other seemed to be genuinely elated that the war was over and considered that after a time Britain, in particular, would accept that it had an obligation to all Monarchies (except Germany). She also seemed to be very pleased that the Kaiser had been forced into exile also. There is no reference to the Hapsburgs here. The Grand Duke is not quoted but Olga is quoted as listening very carefully to her parents and being upset and "shedding tears" with her sisters that it was all over without a victory for their country.

Dinner that evening was a celebration of sorts "they all partook of a little red wine excepting His M who did not eat his meal."

DECEMBER 18, 1918

Tomorrow we take leave of this house and place and start upon the journey to the southern shore. At last the plan is set and we go this way despite all other word sent to you. To Kungar to Simbirsk to Kvalynsk when we change horses so to speak then on to Tambov to Pavloska to Ekaterino to Kherson to Sebastopol to Odessa. Then all is in the hand of God for who can tell whence they will be taken.

Odessa seems a far cry but there the Frenchmen will help their British ally.

It is now below freezing temperature outside and snow covers roads and trees alike. We do not know of weather conditions along the way.

His M rejoices and the G.D.s likewise. Now our time is come Her M seems not to be satisfied and asks about the conveyances of which we can tell but little saving for the first leg.

When you next may hear is now in the hand of God.

How characteristic of Alexandra! For weeks she had been naggingly impatient to get away, but now that the great moment had arrived "Her Majesty seems not to be satisfied." As we shall see, security problems made them skip some of the places on this itinerary like Sebastopol. They skirted around the outskirts of others, being fearful of recognition among the city crowds. Actually, Kungar, Simbirsk, Tambov and Kherson were substantial towns or cities at the time.

In their passage near Simbirsk there was an especial irony which may have escaped them. This city is now named Ulyanovsk in honor of Vladimir Ilyich Ulyanov Lenin. The guiding spirit of the Soviet Revolution was born there on April 9, 1870, on a hill over-looking the Volga. What a sight for Mother Volga it must have been to see the beardless Nicholas pass by and into total eclipse — the principal victim of a local boy who had long languished in one of the Czar's Siberian jails.

DECEMBER 30, 1918

Arrived Kungar. Journey bad. Snow and slipping on ice. With us ten men of arms. Two servants. Four more who travel first [and who are] armed too. Food bad provided by Field Kitchens as agreed. Sickness for all but G.D. Olga on Christmas Day. Her M much dissatisfied with her Motor so guard made bed within it wherein she travels by herself.

His M kind to all and walks each day with first guard [and] al-though this makes the Chief of the Staff anxious [it] is good for [morale of the] men.

Two miles from Kungar to South is our resting place. The camp is good as such things go and fires had been lighted. Officer quarters. Two days ago before we got to here a fire broke out and caused some inquiry from the town as camp believed abandoned. Two extra nights on road not good.

We go on to Simbirsk at day break.

JANUARY 20, 1919 *(Not Verbatim)*

They stayed in Kungar for three days and did not depart as planned because some miles to the south the roads were impass-able. They were in a disused army camp and as food supplies were only provided for one night they had to eat what was described as "iron rations" provided for the journey. As these had to be replaced it meant going into Kungar where there was hardly any food anyway. But from farms and so on the Russian guards managed to get eggs, fresh milk and hams. They also got flour for bread and baked this but later on it says they were eating this same bread when it was moldy. The Empress was genuinely ill and the reporter is much too delicate to describe the illness except to refer to vomiting and "attendant expulsions." When they got away the guard was reduced from a total of fourteen to twelve because two of the Japanese were too ill to travel.

They by-passed Simbirsk because the town was not under the control of the Soviet Government [at this point the term "provisional" government has been dropped and now it is called the Soviet Government]. They were ten miles from the town on the 14th and stayed outside it — again at a disused army camp — because the Emperor had flu again and the Empress refused to allow him to be moved on. He had of course stopped his daily walks with the guards and Tatiana was doing this instead.

They got to Kvalynsk on the 20th by which time the Emperor has got over his flu, the weather is cold but clear and there seems to be no security problem.

JANUARY 31, 1919 *(Not Verbatim)*

When they left Kvalynsk things were much better. The Japanese stayed with them and were joined by eight American civilians with marine training as well as four more Russians making a total of twenty-four guards, two servants, plus two U. S. Government Agents [one of which is the narrator we have had all through]. They had three trucks, four cars, good food supplies and three cases of Whiskey. (This was carefully rationed out among everyone and everyone drank it.) The Empress continued to have a car to herself, grumbled the whole time about cold and had extra blankets taken from the other cars. There seemed to have been no incidents worth reporting on the journey to Tambov which I gather was pretty slow.

At Tambov they stayed at a private house — "private dwelling mansion of good proportions"—where they were comfortable and well looked after. The Empress started doing some crochet work again [which must be some of the most valuable sewing of all time if it still exists]. The Emperor is busy talking in German and trying hard to perfect his accent and the same guard who was teaching him in Siberia is in the party. The two servants are helped in their work by the Russian guards. The Japanese do not seem much disposed to anything except their exact job of going ahead, in turns with the Russians, to make sure all is well.

The house at Tambov seems to have been very well equipped. The beds are "soft and of great comfort to us all and the linen clean smelling unlike anything we have known for many a long month." The date they arrived was three days before the date of this dispatch and so I calculate they spent four nights here. [The dispatch says they are leaving next day.]

FEBRUARY 9, 1919 *(Not Verbatim)*

They had to travel day and night from Tambov to Kherson where they arrived at this date. The roads were good, the military situation less so. Also they had received word that the French were going to ignore them when they got to Odessa. During this journey the sender of the cables spent some time walking with the Emperor who discussed the future of Monarchies and said he did not think many would survive for more than twenty-five years and probably very much less. He anticipated that the British throne would be the next to go and that Britain would soon be governed by a Soviet like his own Country. He did not think this would happen in Germany which he seemed to think might even take back the Kaiser. Equally he thought that the Jews would take over America through a Soviet uprising. He seems to be very anti-semitic in that he regards the Soviets as being Jewish run and financed and seeking world domination. He also said that he did not think the Allied Invasion would do any good [I presume this was the Allied invasion of Russia]. I gathered from this report that they did not stop for anything except "necessities" in their anxiety to get to the "Southern Shores" as quickly as possible.

Fed by field kitchens. More Whiskey. Stayed in Camp at Kherson. Empress sitting up in car. Emperor walking again with guards. Also Girls travelling in trucks with Japanese Guards. No mention of Grand Duke. Weather conditions good. Fighting going on all around. Could not stop at two of the staging posts because of lack of security.

FEBRUARY 17, 1919

And now it is the time for me to write a last dispatch in triumph. All, as you know, has gone well to plan. The journey [is] over and if the risks were big the consequence [are] more than rewarding.

From the empty Monastery at the last [staging] post ten miles south towards Odessa from Kherson where the planned way was changed from Sevastapol to this city the way was untroubled save for the hour when we crossed over into Allied Command protection. The place was barren and we could not wait for fear of causing such suspicion [that] we'd be searched so there we retracked and came at a fine speed along the road with no cover, all the engines working well. No questioning or examining of credentials. Then on to Odessa where some fighting was going on within the streets but not to cause us to change the way.

At the Officials house commandeered by America for our [their] staff we found little preparation had been made. We were given shelter as though we were all Americans with Russian families and friends. His M and Her M sharing one good bedroom and two American guards sharing with the G.D. The G.D.s, all four, shared a small room with a splendid view of all the harbor.

Fed well and cared for, hot bath water being the luxury of life, warm and safe, they waited there til last night. The Russian guards made off the day before and our Asian friends left us at the post before the crossing into this safer territory.

His M would not permit his family to stray from the residence but to our despair yesterday to Church they did insist upon to attend. This Church of the Archangel is much attended by the people and their disguise is not true camouflage. All would insist on attending and thus they went. First His M with the G.D.s O and T. Then Her M with the G.D. Then the two young G.D.s. They stayed apart from each group and returned separately too. If they were known no signal has been given.

At 11 o'clock in the night many people as well as sailors are at the wharf and many tenders. They boarded the small boat after walking to the wharf. The signal given they moved out into the dark water toward the British ship lying in wait and [all] prepared. Goodbye was said at the residence and the journey to this Southern shore (now completed) all were moved to gratitude and some to tears, relief and respectful affection mixing.

I am asked to say the code name by which the telegraphs were sent is now to be discarded and as no message will come from me again for I shall have no word. I shall not leave here until I am ordered to another duty.

A "holy mess" is about the calmest description of Odessa given by witnesses in late 1918 and early 1919. The picturesque port on the Black Sea, on the south shore of a semi-circular bay, had been taken by the Ukrainian Rada (legislature) after the overthrow of the Kerensky regime. Then in rapid succession, it was seized by the Bolsheviks, the Germans, the Ukrainians again, and the French. Helping the French were the British, Poles, Greeks, Romanians and Serbs. During this Allied intervention, in the late fall of 1918, the British Navy figured prominently and the city was bombarded.

When the Romanovs passed through, there was an uneasy truce among the shoreside factions. A French general tried to maintain order among a dozen cliques of Whites, Ukrainians, Cossacks, Turks, Greeks, Poles, Italians and not-so-secret Red sympathizers. France's own troops and seamen were in a mutinous mood over being engaged in a new fighting front after World War I was over and this eventually caused the French to pull out of the city and go home (but not until after the Romanovs left). The French were succeeded, first by a second Soviet Government and then, in April 1919, by White forces under General Anton Ivanovich Deniken.

At the time of the Romanovs' brief visit, the French were so desperate for peace-keeping forces in the seething city that they were glad to accept the services as military police of defeated German soldiers who were in need of food, and had been searching all over the Crimea for someone to accept their surrender. This produced some grotesque scenes around the waterfront bars — carousing and disorderly Allied servicemen finding themselves arrested by a despised "Heinie," a breed which they thought their own forces had vanquished weeks before on the Western Front.

But of all the scenes in Odessa in those days, history may choose as the most grotesque, dramatic and meaningful the passage of the last Imperial Family of Russia — disguised as common refugees — down the steps of the wharf's gangway to the tender of the "British ship."

What an event this was to which the secret agents had taken the greatest pains to avoid attracting attention!

It was a signal landmark in the 300-year-old story of a strange and colorful dynasty. It was a cairn, a signpost, a boundary marker for Nicholas, his wife and children, but the chances are that it came to mean something quite different to the harried and beardless ex-Czar than it did to his offspring. For him it may have marked the gateway to a peaceful, private existence for which he had long been yearning. Perhaps he vowed to his rescuers that he would never surface again for the rest of his life. As ward of the revolutionists at Tsarskoe Selo and Tobolsk, he had shown flashes of quiet pleasure that the court charade was over; that at last he was a private person who could take time to read *David Copperfield* aloud to Marie, to meditate, to chop wood, to commune with his beloved trees. By the time he reached Odessa, he must have been a man without any more illusions of grandeur. A brief look at the chaos in that port which the French were trying to organize must have been a poor invitation to him or anyone else of his age to return to public life.

But for his children, that wharf, that departure from Russian soil, marked the entrance into new eras of emotional tumult which few other persons can ever have experienced. The years ahead of them, in direst anonymity, were to create something of an epic for lives that ranged from one extreme of fortune to another. Save for Alexandra, the last of the reigning Romanovs had lived from the days of infancy at the summit of the world's largest and richest autocracy. By those who surrounded them they were flattered, coddled, cajoled, waited on, kowtowed to and entreated for the most trifling favors.

And then everything was changed. They were on the run. Their empire was gone. They were hiding like hunted thieves. They had sacrificed their story book castles, their costumery, their privileges. They had to learn to act like outcasts. One wrong move, one slip of the tongue, and they knew they would have to pay the penalty of being natural targets of vengeance from unnumbered victims of the cruelties of the Okhrana, the Czarist secret police, or from anyone who had a grudge against the regime. They had to steel themselves to react to everything quite differently from the ways in which they had been taught lest a courtly gesture betray them. And as year after year passed and every hope proved unfounded that their masquerade could end, one tolerance after another must have snapped, one facet of personality after another gone numb.

In the search that any normal person makes to find others to confide in, others capable of understanding and sympathizing, how chilling the effects must have been to realize that the truth rarely could be risked to anyone — that for the most part one must go on acting out a living fraud.

In the end, how much of any of the original identities were left?

How much of what remained was synthetic overlay, spiritual skin graft, mere camouflage that matured into make-believe people who had recreated themselves in plastic/surgery style until they were as uncertain as everyone else about their own real identity?

CHAPTER 8

LORD HARDINGE'S LETTER

The trail of the Romanovs in the Chivers Papers ends at Odessa, but is immediately picked up by another document, also unearthed by Peter Bessell, from the White House archives — the "Lord Hardinge Letter." According to Bessell, he was allowed to hand-copy its contents on a visit to the White House in March, 1973 and shortly afterwards received an accurate, typewritten transcript. Bessell also informed me that a photocopy of the letter had been given to the British foreign office who had found no reason to suspect forgery, although no copy could be found on file in London. I have never been able to confirm Mr. Bessell's story. It is through this letter, however, that Jeremy Thorpe publicly broached the issue of the rescue in London, an indication that he believed its authenticity.

Lord Hardinge's letter to King George V of England defines the escape route from Odessa, and synchronizes in time and place with the Chivers Papers.

Lord Hardinge was introduced to the reader in Chapter Six. A former Viceroy of India as well as Ambassador to Russia, he had been a great favorite of George V's father, Edward VII, had written many of the latter's speeches and accompanied him on foreign tours. He was a close confidante of the Royal Family. Here is the text of his letter to George V:

(Foreign Office seal)
From Lord Hardinge of Penshurst, Permanent Under Secretary for Foreign Affairs
3* June, 1919
The King
Your Majesty,

In response to Your Majesty's enquiry, I have ascertained from the Chargé d'Affaires Vienna that the route taken by His Imperial Majesty the Czar and the Grand Duchesses Olga, Tatiana and Marie was as you were informed by Her Majesty the Queen Mother.

From Odessa to Constantinople arriving February 26.

From Constantinople by train arriving Sofia February 28.

From Sofia to Wien on March 3, arriving Wien March 7.

From Wien to Linz by car arriving March 8.

From Linz to Wroclaw, or Breslau, on May 6, arriving Wroclaw, May 10.

I am,

Your Majesty's Servant,

Hardinge of P.

*The numeral in the original is indistinct and may read 5 or 8.

The time and substance of this report call for a little orientation. "Her Majesty the Queen Mother" mentioned in the first paragraph is Queen Alexandra, Danish-born mother of George V. Less than a month before, on May 9, she had greeted her sister Marie, mother of Nicholas II, after the British battleship *Lord Nelson* had completed the last lap of the Dowager Empress's voyage from the Crimea. She was the next to last of the first magnitude Romanovs to be evacuated in 1919. The last was Marie's daughter, the Grand Duchess Olga, with her commoner husband and two young sons.

After the welcoming ceremonies were over at Portsmouth it would have been quite natural for the two sisters to compare notes on the latest news of Nicholas, Alexandra and their five children. The Lord Hardinge letter suggests that Marie had given her sister all the facts about the secret escape route which had been passed on to her during her stopover at the San Antonio Palace in Malta.

Alexandra would have told her son, King George. Knowing that his mother was quite deaf and often misunderstood what was said to her, he doubtless would have asked Lord Hardinge to check it out through Foreign Office sources. Hence the letter. It clearly states that it is a response to the King's "enquiry."

Note also that, according to Lord Hardinge, only four of the seven Romanovs made the trip from Constantinople to Breslau. That leaves an important trio to be accounted for — Alexandra and Alexei, both in delicate health at the time, and Anastasia. What became of them?

An educated guess is that they were left in a hospital or sanitarium somewhere in Romania or Bulgaria. Indeed, it is not unlikely that Constantinople was inserted in the intelligence reports as a diversion for security purposes. The Turks detested the Romanovs and the latter would have been in dire peril if news of their presence leaked out in the purlieus of the Golden Horn. Likewise, if news came that Romania or Bulgaria was giving aid and comfort, there might have been Bolshevik counteraction at the level of lower Red ranks. Both countries were fearful that the Bolshevik Revolution would spill across their borders.

Thus, if the Bulgarian Version is right, there is a chance that all seven Romanovs spent longer in Bulgaria than the dossiers show, under the protection of Nicholas's godson, King Boris III, and that the four who proceeded to Breslau in the spring of 1919 actually spent less time in Austria than the schedule indicates.

After mentioning Vienna once, Lord Hardinge then refers to it by its better-known European name of "Wien." Who was the "Chargé d'Affaires Vienna" whom he consulted about the Romanovs' route, as stated in the first paragraph of his letter?

The Foreign Office lists for 1918 and 1919 are not much help. They show no chargé d'affaires in Vienna until much later. They indicate that most of the incoming reports from Vienna in 1919 were signed by "Colonel Sir T. Cuninghame, British Military Representative." Most probably Colonel Cuninghame doubled as British Chargé d'Affaires at the time. It was not until January, 1920 that a Briton (Lindsay) took over the Vienna post as "His Majesty's High Commissioner." The Americans were also represented there in 1919 by a military man, a Captain Gregory. Those were painful days for the hungry and defeated Austrians who were trying to transform the "empty elegance" of a Habsburg empire into a parliamentary government. The Reds were waiting in the wings.

Linz, a railroad center on the Danube, was then Austrian and so remains. In Nazi Germany it was best-known for the fact that Adolf Hitler fretfully endured his early schooldays there, and got rather poor marks, too. Breslau was then German, but later became part of the German slice awarded to Poland after World War II.

There was a splendid Habsburg estate about twenty-four miles outside of Linz. If the Austrian authorities were cooperative, it would have been just right as a hideout for the Romanovs. It offered both imperial splendor and privacy. It had superb landscaping and a fine view, and for years had belonged to Archduke Hubert Salvator and his wife, Rosemary, Princess of Salm-Salm. It was called "Wallsee." The Romanovs could have spent a few precious weeks in it under the illusion that they were back in one of their palaces and that nothing had changed, even though the sixty-six-year-long reign of Emperor Franz Josef had expired less than three years before.

There is a final irony about the Lord Hardinge letter and its role in solving the case. The letter most definitely seems to have been provoked by the coming to England of Nicholas's mother, the one figure whose dichotomous accounts of her son's family maintained to the day of her death — but always off-the-record — that none were assassinated.

She left strong clues all along her route: on the battleship *Marlborough* which picked her up at Yalta; at Malta, where she was gay and the life of all the parties held for her, and aboard the battleship *Lord Nelson* which carried her on the final stage of her trip to England.

Nowhere and at no time did she act like a bereaved mother and grandmother.

At Malta, in the San Antonio Palace, she attended a testimonial luncheon in her honor and twenty-two persons were seated at table. Next to her was a young aide, a British Army lieutenant, Robert Ingham. Later he wrote:

"Her Majesty chatted freely with me during the luncheon and talked about her relatives and the awful time they had in Russia . . . so I was rather surprised when Her Majesty began to talk about her son — the Czar — and told me she was being careful not to let others know, but that *she* knew where he was. H.I.M. was fully convinced that he had escaped and was in hiding at a certain place."

Her debonair mood prevailed on the *Lord Nelson*. Georgina Battiscombe, in an epilogue to her book on Queen Alexandra, describes how the officers of that homeward-bound vessel were, to their amazement, routed out of their sleeping quarters one night at sea and ordered to appear on deck in proper uniform for dancing. Dowager Empress Marie, it was explained to them, had decreed that they all should have a ball. She had found the night utterly bewitching.

Certainly these were not the reactions of a woman in mourning.

Hindsight now informs us that Nicholas's mother was flying her own signals on the case for years before her death in 1928. It is remarkable how few persons heeded those signals. She could be the most surprised of all, if she had lived, to discover that it was the information given to her sister, and confirmed by Lord Hardinge, which would have to wait fifty-five years to become public.

There is a very human epilogue to the discovery of the Lord Hardinge letter. Before the Foreign Office validated it to the best of its ability, according to Mr. Bessell, the letter brought diverse reactions from the few scholars and diplomats who had had a chance to study it. All were expert in the customs of Whitehall.

One retired veteran of the British diplomatic service said that he found one thing "suspect" about the letter. It was its references to Vienna in both English and German spellings, all in the space of a few paragraphs.

"I doubt," he said, "that a professional diplomat like Lord Hardinge would have used the German word for Vienna, 'Wien.' All official British correspondence that I have seen on the subject always uses the English version, 'Vienna.'"

But Lord Hardinge's use of "Wien" was precisely what another evaluator, a British history scholar, considered an especially authentic touch. Said he:

"It is quite right that Vienna, rather than Wien or Vien, is embedded in the vernacular of Britons and British diplomacy. That is why Lord Hardinge used it in his first paragraph when he mentioned 'the Chargé d'Affaires Vienna.'

"But at that point in his correspondence to the King he had a decision to make. Obviously, from the text of the letter, the King had sent him an itinerary to check out. Its source was the Queen Mother. Her source most likely was her sister, the Dowager Empress. Both were Danish born.

"If the King, in forwarding the itinerary to Lord Hardinge for a checkout, had chosen to leave the itinerary as it was given to him, including 'Wien' spelled as it was, should he change it, in sending it back to the King?

"Does one correct or rewrite one's seniors? Does one risk offending one's Monarch with an implied criticism of his use or his mother's or aunt's use of the German spelling? I should rather imagine not. I would imagine that Lord Hardinge made a decision in consonance with his diplomatic training. He used the English spelling in what was basically his own paragraph. I mean the first one. He used the German spelling as it had come to him in what were basically paragraphs from the King or the Queen Mother.

"A forger, not comprehending these nuances, would not have thought to use both 'Vienna' and 'Wien' in the same short letter. It should be recalled, too, that German was frequently spoken at the Windsor Court."

In the all-enveloping mystery of the Romanovs, this clash of opinion shows what one small word can do to produce completely opposite conclusions among sophisticated bystanders.

Likewise, it was a revelation to note how a few Britons quite

sure of their knowledge of the ways of the court worked themselves into a lather of skepticism over what they regarded as Lord
Hardinge's levity of tone in this letter. They contended that it
couldn't be authentic because it lacked the kind of literary genu-
flection that they would expect the diplomat to display, they said,
in writing to his king. Other Britons disagree with him, and so do I.
Considering the brevity of the missive and its factual nature, and
considering Lord Hardinge's long intimacy with the Windsors, the
contents seem fully respectful and believable.

CHAPTER 9

THE BULGARIAN INTERLUDE

A decision by King Ferdinand of Bulgaria, before the turn of the century, laid the basis for what is now the Bulgarian Version of the rescue of the Romanovs. It conforms in general with the Chivers Papers and Lord Hardinge's Letter, but goes into far greater detail about the fate of the Imperial Family after leaving Odessa.

The Bulgarian part of the story presented here lacks certain fine embroidery in respect to the locale of the hideaway, because the documentation is in the custody of the Bulgarian Orthodox Church and a small group of Bulgarian expatriates. They haven't yet decided among themselves how or when, if ever, to make them public. I am grateful that one of them was good enough to pass along to me the essential facts.

By the testimony of these facts, it was indeed a prophetic decision of the 1890s, made in the royal palace at Sofia, that set the mould for the Bulgarian Version now emerging almost four generations later. This was the determination by the German-born King Ferdinand, a Roman Catholic, to seek a rapprochement with

Russia by having his son and heir, Boris, brought up in the Orthodox Church. It was an act of statesmanship made for the benefit of Bulgaria, which often trembled on the flanks of its giant neighbor. Ferdinand never could have dreamed that some day it would turn out to be a merciful bit of luck for the cause of all the trembling — the Czar himself.

Ferdinand's overtures in respect to his son's religious future were well-received in St. Petersburg. As a result, in elaborate ceremonies on Feb. 14, 1896, Nicholas II became the infant Boris's godfather. As a secondary result, the ex-Czar Nicholas II in the dark hours of his life in late 1918 found at least one happy consolation. The newly-installed young King Boris of Bulgaria was his godson and coreligionist. By all the vows and bonds of their church, the young monarch owed his godfather all the help he could render short of provoking the Reds to invade his small nation. It was also obvious to all concerned that whatever was going to be done for the Romanovs in Bulgaria must be kept a very dark secret.

The central figure of the Bulgarian Version was a sensitive and intelligent young man with dark blue eyes, dark hair and a slim figure. He had the narrow, pale face of an ascetic. This was King Boris III. He was named for a predecessor who converted the kingdom to Christianity in A.D. 865. Toward the end of 1918, King Boris III was twenty-four. He had been on the throne only a few weeks following his father's abdication on October 4.

The gift of a sanctuary to the Romanovs came at an uneasy and melancholy period for Bulgaria. King Ferdinand had bet wrong on his military alignment in World War I and the country was paying a heavy price for it. He had allied his kingdom with the Germans. His abdication on the eve of a general armistice in Europe was his tacit admission of the mistake. Few monarchs had experienced a more up-and-down, success-and-failure, run of fortune. With the help of Russia and Romania, his nation had cut loose from five hundred years of vassalage in the crumbling Ottoman Empire.

Maximilian Karl Leopold Maria Ferdinand saw his mission as one of building Bulgaria into the greatest power in the Balkans, and for a while he succeeded. He was the fifth and youngest son of

Prince Augustus of Saxe-Coburg and Gotha. He was born on Feb. 26, 1861. His travels with his brother, Augustus, in South America whetted his interest in the natural sciences, and a volume of their joint botanical studies was published in Vienna in 1883. Later he swung into a military career, and he was a lieutenant in an Austrian hussar regiment when he was elected to the title of a Prince of Bulgaria and placed in charge of the government at Sofia in 1887. So well did he apply his knowledge of military tactics to his new country's fighting forces that by the early 1900s Bulgaria had one of the best armies in Southeast Europe.

It was Ferdinand who conceived of forming the Balkan League which included Bulgaria, Greece, Serbia and Montenegro in 1911, and when the league became a military coalition the following year, it was a string of victories by the Bulgarian Army that enabled those countries to win a war against Turkey in 1912. The victory vastly augmented Bulgaria's territory. A year later, however, Ferdinand lost almost all the gains of 1912, including the province of Macedonia, after some members of the Balkan League became bitter rivals. In 1913, Turkey was induced to join Montenegro, Serbia and Greece in attacking Bulgaria. The kingdom was faced by four enemies at the same time. She had to capitulate. In the Treaty of Bucharest, which ended the new hostilities in 1913, Bulgaria surrendered Macedonia to the Serbians and Greeks, among many other trophies of 1912. It was the Kaiser's promise to help restore these trophies that led Ferdinand to join the Central Powers in World War I.

Once more the Bulgarians won a row of victories — in Macedonia, Thrace and Romania. And once more, with the overall defeat of the Central Powers in Europe, it availed them nothing but a heavy list of casualties. It added up to more than enough disappointment for any king in one lifetime, and so it proved, indeed, for Ferdinand. The very evening of the October day that he abdicated, he left Sofia for a long retirement in Coburg. There must have been an additional touch of remorse for him in his relations with the son who succeeded him. Boris had served dutifully as an army officer in the wars of 1912 and 1913. He had put in long hours on his father's staff in World War I, and all during those years, his father knew very well, he had found nothing to alter his disapproval of Bulgaria's alliance with Germany.

This fact proved to be an asset for Boris in the early months of his reign. His countrymen knew how he felt about the Germans. More than seventy per cent of them, it was reported, had the same view from the very start of the war.

As for the Russians, they might have been more unpopular in Bulgaria at the time if the two countries had been joined by a common border, but there was a buffer state between them — Romania. Its better-educated, more cosmopolitan peoples, with their merciless air of superiority, long had been rivals of the Bulgarians for supremacy in Balkan affairs. Many Bulgarians regarded these close neighbors as treacherous and invariably self-seeking. In 1912, the Romanians had remained aloof from the Balkan League, but had managed to benefit from the military successes of its members against the Turks. The very next year the Romanians ganged up with the Turks and others to attack Bulgaria.

Again, in the second full year of World War I (1916), when the Allied cause looked promising and the chance for regional territorial gains beckoned, Romania became a combatant against the Central Powers and Bulgaria — only to suffer ignominious defeats and make an early withdrawal.

Whereas Russia, as seen from the palace windows in Sofia, was a different cup of tea altogether. Often annoying, and sometimes fearsome, the land of the czars had continually played the protective role of big brother to Bulgaria in maintaining her posture of hostility to her big league rival on the Turkish Straits — the Ottoman Empire. Older Bulgarians could well remember the help rendered by St. Petersburg when she had shaken loose their country from the Sultans, in the Russian war against the Turks in 1877 and 1878, and had won the guarantee of Bulgaria's independence by the Treaties of San Stefano and Berlin. To the pious farmers of Bulgaria, as well as to their monarch, peering northward over the Romanian fence, the pious peasants of Russia didn't seem as forbidding as a lot of other foreigners, even though they had been titular enemies in World War I. And the dethroned Nicholas II had a number of things going for him in the Bulgarian capital. He had been an ally of the victorious Allies; thus he was a friend of the winners and could be influential with President Wilson and the peacemakers. He and his family had powerful relatives in several European courts. He was a potential rallying point for any anti-Communist crusade which the great powers might feel obliged to organize against the Bolsheviks and, if such a thing ever material-ized, it was not inconceivable that Bulgaria would join it.

But the matter of giving sanctuary to Nicholas had its negative aspects, too. Should news of it ever leak out, it could draw counter-measures from the Reds. These could be serious if Britain, France, Italy and the United States withdrew their naval units from the Black Sea, and the navy of Lenin and Trotsky won free access to the Bulgarian coast. Furthermore, there were pro-Russian factions in Bulgaria. The most potent of these were persons of Macedonian origin. If they were won over to the Bolshevik cause there could be hell to pay.

Clearly the maintenance of secrecy about the Romanovs' visit was the most important feature of the whole operating plan.

That was the situation in its time setting, according to the Bul-garian Version, as the small British merchantman carrying the beardless Nicholas and the well-disguised members of his family steamed from Odessa to Burgas, the ancient seaport of Pyrgos, on the Bulgarian shore of the Black Sea. It is about 300 miles from Odessa. At a cruising speed of fifteen knots, the trip would take about twenty hours.

The Romanovs' royal host — King Boris III — was still a bach-elor. Only a poet of the first magnitude could do justice to the thoughts which must have passed through his mind as he realized that one of the first duties of his office was to give a secret welcome to a man who had not only been Czar of all the Russias, but who had been his own godfather in a ceremony performed when he was too young to remember it.

Scholarly and shy as he was at this time of his life, the young King of Bulgaria was no recluse. He had done well in the national military academy and in the army. He spoke several languages. He was almost as conversant in botany as his father. He had travelled widely in the Mediterranean with a Swiss tutor and a Bulgarian professor, and had gone to London in 1911 to attend the coronation of King George V. He had spent enjoyable weeks sightseeing in Brussels and Paris.

Though several sciences interested him, mechanics were his principal hobby. He was proud of the fact that he could dismantle and reassemble the engine of a Rolls Royce. He was amused by the nickname he had picked up: "The royal chauffeur." He had become very close to his brother and two sisters, who had been obliged to make their own family life following the premature death of their mother, Princess Marie Louise of Bourbon Parma, in 1899. His constant companion, indeed, was one of his sisters, Princess Eudoxie.

One wonders what must have passed through Eudoxie's head as she pondered the likely effects on her brother of the advent of four very eligible former grand duchesses of Russia, all minus their Tsarskoe Selo wardrobes, all once the favorites of the fashion editors of four continents.

It's a fair guess that the "large country house" in which the Bulgarian Version hides the Romanovs for their stay in King Boris's domain was somewhere in the area around Burgas. Otherwise, one presumes, they would have been disembarked in the more northerly Bulgarian port of Varna, which is much nearer to Odessa.

Burgas was the center of a centuries-old holidaying region. All around the Gulf of Burgas, hotels, resorts and residences on the hills and beaches had long exploited the local benisons of a warm winter sun and cool summer breezes. It was a favored health spot in the days of the Roman Empire. The Romans built one of their great imperial cities, Anchialus, at the head of the gulf. Mineral springs about seven miles from the present harbor of Burgas were renowned as far back as the Fourth Century under the Latin title of "Aqua Callidae."

Burgas is less than sixty miles from the Turkish border. The insertion of Constantinople in the Lord Hardinge report for this stage of the Romanovs' journey, if it was a dissimilation for security purposes, didn't put the travellers very far off course. The railroad from Constantinople to Vienna runs lengthwise through Bulgaria and traverses the basins and valleys of the southern hill country not far from Burgas.

The Bulgarian Version puts the Romanovs' hideout in an estate used by a military force of Bulgarian insurgents in the late 1940s and early 1950s as a headquarters. There were some records, as well as local reports, of the Romanovs' stopover in and around the place, and when some of the insurgents later bolted to the West, they brought the stories with them. This led to further investigation by outsiders to whom the whole episode was a brand new lead on the Romanov Case.

No matter how long different members of the Imperial Family stayed in Bulgaria, Austria, Germany, Poland or elsewhere, their ultimate shelter in the years of underground existence, according to the Bulgarian Version, was Belgium. This can be entirely wrong, of course, or only partly true. The Bulgarians claim that the Romanovs became wards of King Albert and Queen Elizabeth of the Belgians, the famed pair who refused to capitulate to the Kaiser's armies and made a point of living close to their troops in World War I's hectic years of retreats and advances.

But when the Romanovs left their own country, the Bulgarian churchmen had no guarantees that such intelligence as reached them about the fate of Nicholas and his family in the underground of other nations was anything more than hearsay. There are reports in Bulgaria that Nicholas wrote letters back to one or two prelates of the church. If so, I have not been able to track them down.

The Bulgarian Version has Nicholas dying in Belgium in 1952, a year before the death of Stalin. That is the same year given in the version of Lt. Col. Michal Goleniewski, the defector from Polish military intelligence who came out of the cold of East Berlin in 1960. But Goleniewski claims that Nicholas died in Poland and was buried in the little parish cemetery of Wolsztyn under the name of "Michal Goleniewski." If the exiled Romanovs split up after 1920, it is more than likely that no one well-versed in the Bulgarian part of the story has any idea what finally became of them.

What is the likely credibility of that Belgian dénouement?

Princess Marina Kropotkin, another exile from Czarist Russia as a girl of seven, was also taken under the wing of Elizabeth, the Belgian Queen, after World War I. Now the mother of grown children, Princess Kropotkin lives in Bedford Hills, New York.

"It is quite true," she told me, "that Queen Elizabeth went out of her way to look out for members or relatives of court families who were having a hard time.

"I was one of the fortunate young people for whom she set up funds or scholarships or both in Belgium. There were twenty or thirty others, I believe, at the time. The Queen also provided homes for Empress Zita of Austria and her children, for relatives of the Pretender to the Throne of France, and others in that category.

"They made up a dispersed community in the small but attractive chateaux that the Queen maintained around Bruges, near the North Sea. I know that one of my second cousins, Nicolai Obolensky, and his children, were the Queen's guests at the Abbey of St. Andries, near Bruges. If the Romanovs were among those present it is certainly news to me. It is not by any means impossible, however. Those were troubled times. I was just a child then — no one knew everyone and everything. Few people asked questions about the past. The future was problem enough for all of us."

CHAPTER 10

STRATEGY AND TACTICS

In the context of the statecraft of 1918, historians who search deeply enough may have to admit that the planning and execution of the rescue become far more logical, indeed, far more understandable, than the mass murder of the Romanovs which the Bolsheviks reported.

The key to the riddle is what happened in late 1917 and early 1918 in the old fortress city of Brest-Litovsk, near the Russo-Polish border. It was there, on March 3, 1918, that the Bolsheviks signed a separate peace treaty with Germany and the Central Powers which took Russia out of the war.

But in the weeks before the signing there had been fruitless bargaining and dickering among the negotiators. That followed a December 5 armistice. In January, Lenin sent Trotsky, his commissar of foreign affairs, to deal with the triumphant invaders. Each side wanted peace, but each side's terms were unacceptable to the other. The Bolsheviks wanted a breathing space to consolidate their gains in the turmoil of their home front. The Germans wanted to free two million men from their Eastern Front in order to win the race against U.S. reinforcement arriving in the West.

The fiery Trotsky found the German terms intolerable. He waved his arms and made speeches while the German diplomats yawned and their generals fingered their sidearms.

Finally, and for the second time, Trotsky walked out of the Brest-Litovsk conference. The date was February 10, 1918.

The Germans' response was swift. They repudiated the armistice. They invaded Estonia. Their troops reached the outskirts of Petrograd. Lenin came to the desperate realization that Bolshevism would soon be crushed completely, and Russia along with it, unless he reached a pact with the aggressors. Being a good psychologist, furthermore, he didn't send the irritating Trotsky back to face the Germans at Brest-Litovsk. He sued for an armistice again and dispatched a new figure to head the Russian delegation in the negotiations. This was Gregory Y. Sokolnikov, another member of the Central Committee. His orders, apparently, were to agree to almost anything, and that is exactly what he did. The terms of the signed treaty were much stiffer than those which Trotsky had rejected.

Fifty-two years later in London, one of Brest-Litovsk's most interesting provisions was uncovered by Peter Bessell's researcher. It is the secret codicil in the treaty by which the Reds agreed to a German stipulation that "safe passage" be granted to the Imperial Family of Russia. It is one of the most natural paragraphs in the world. The Kaiser was in a position to demand that his cousins be given their freedom.

Though he may or may not have deplored the Romanov codicil as one of the prices he had to pay for a peace with Germany, Lenin probably valued its secrecy. He may have insisted on it. He knew well that many of his followers wanted to stage a public trial of "Citizen Romanov" for his "crimes against humanity," after which, of course, the guilt being guaranteed in advance, the defendant would be shot. Lenin knew that any word of the "safe passage" concession would cause angry mutterings among the Bolsheviks, bestir outcries from the more militantly anti-Czarist district Soviets like those in Omsk and Ekaterinburg and further endanger the lives of the Romanovs themselves. That, in turn, risked a resumption of the German invasion.

That is the factual background of events for which the Chivers Papers now offer an exciting new epilogue.

After Brest-Litovsk, as Lenin conferred on the next Romanov moves with Yakov Sverdlov (for whom Ekaterinburg was renamed Sverdlovsk), the highest administrative officer of the regime as President of the all-Russian Central Executive Committee, it is by no means fantastic to imagine Lenin speaking like this:

"Safe passage, indeed! It's easy to talk about, but how do we deliver? There they are, those Romanovs, way out in Tobolsk, in Siberia. We didn't put them there. Kerensky did. Any direction you move them will bring them through towns or cities where assassins will be glad to try their luck on them. They'll be ducks in a shooting gallery. Their deaths could put us back to war with the Germans.

"Look, Yakov, we'll need help from the Germans. We'll need help from the British, who have more secret agents here than flies on a dead fish. We'll need help from anyone and everyone who can give it. Why shouldn't we ask for it? The Romanovs are not only related to the Kaiser. They're related to King George. They're kin of the King of Greece and the Queen of Romania. Let's get all of them to work with us. And meantime, or course, Yakov — not a word of it to anyone!"

Sverdlov promptly sent to Tobolsk a secret agent of his own. He was the courtly and mysterious "Sailor on Horseback," Vasily Vaslevich Yakovlev. He took with him 150 picked horsemen and a private telegrapher to enable him to communicate with the Kremlin in code. (Since the German invasion scare near Petrograd, Lenin had moved his government to Moscow.) Yakovlev's mission, according to three historical writers, was either to move the Romanovs where they would have better protection and readier access to the West, or, perhaps, to placate the Germans by making it appear that the Reds were trying to deliver their prisoners to the Kaiser while secretly conniving to have the effort balked.

A great deal of mystification over Yakovlev's role is expressed by writers Edmund A. Walsh, Victor Alexandrov, Robert K. Massie and P. M. Bykov. All devote a lot of space to him. Father Walsh gives him a whole chapter.

Yakovlev arrived in distant Tobolsk on April 22. Whatever his orders really were, his immediate plans went awry from the start. He found the Czarevich Alexei too ill to travel. His parents, taking their daughter, the Grand Duchess Marie, with them, had to leave Alexei behind with his sisters Olga, Tatiana and Anastasia. There came a rough, two-day trip in peasant tarantasses for Yakovlev's imperial party to the nearest railroad station at Tiumen. A train was waiting for them. They started for Omsk, away from Moscow, but soon Yakovlev received a warning from the Omsk Reds, to the east, and the Ekaterinburg Reds, to the west, that his train would not be allowed to pass in either direction. The trap of the anti-Czarists was closing in.

It was then that the canny Sverdlov made a daring gamble. Or so the Chivers Papers imply, though he isn't mentioned in them.

He ordered Yakovlev to deliver the Romanovs to the leaders of the bloodthirsty Ural District Soviet at Ekaterinburg. His logic is now clearer: It would throw them off guard and buy a little time. It would yield a false sense of security to the miners, smelters and metal workers of Ekaterinburg who had been crying for Nicholas's scalp, for they would find themselves rewarded suddenly with the bounty they craved — the Romanovs' live bodies. No longer would they be up in arms over a feeling of being cheated by trickery in the Kremlin. There would be a quiet pause in which their leaders, under orders from Lenin, would have to go through the motions of preparing a trial for Citizen Romanov and, in this process, to maintain all respectable legal appearances, the Kremlin could insist on time-consuming delays.

This would enable the Imperial Family to be fixed in time and place. The big mansion of the rich merchant Ipatiev could be requisitioned (and was). The left-behind Romanov children could be brought on from Tobolsk. All could be put on a predictable schedule in Ipatiev House. Thereafter any kind of an escape could be planned only after the secret agents in the jailbreak plot had a chance to study the locale and familiarize themselves with the big and little buildings, the points of observation, the personalities of the guards, the layout of doors, gates and passageways. At the right moment all the guards could be changed, and they were replaced on July 4 by ten "Letts" of the Bolshevik Cheka.

The Papers prove that Lenin got all the help he needed from foreign agents — and then some. They also prove that a well-staged "assassination" brought a new increment of security to the members of the ill-starred Imperial Family during those queasy days and months before they could make their way out of Russian territory. After all, gunmen don't stalk corpses.

To top it all, the Japanese trading mission was a stroke of genius. Few would have thought that the Japanese were in on it. And if they did, still fewer would have deigned to search that well-guarded hideaway fifteen miles out of town.

It is more than possible that the Japanese Emperor's personal intercession was the repayment of a family debt of honor incurred in 1891, as noted in Chapter Six. That year, Nicholas, as the 23-year-old Czarevich, was making a tour of the Far East. Yoshihito's father, Mutsuhito, better known as the Emperor Meiji, was then on the throne. During a ceremonial appearance at Otsu, near Kyoto, Nicholas was attacked by a member of the Japanese guard. The visiting Russian heir-apparent came close to being killed by a blow on his head. Thereafter he carried a permanent scar on his temple. It was known in his family as the "Otsu mark." It showed a discoloration when he was angry or excited.

The Nipponese have a strong tradition to the effect that "any of us who dishonors himself dishonors us all." Thus, by the same token, the Imperial Family of Japan may have waited 27 years to atone for this offense against the Imperial Family of Russia. During that time Japan had been an implacable enemy of the Czar's empire in one war (the Russo-Japanese War of 1904-05) and an ally in another (World War I).

There is a strong scent of British contrivance about the changing sequence of responsibility in the rescue of the Romanovs — from the Bolsheviks to the Japanese to the Americans to the British. The motto of the British Secret Service in those days was: "When there is a chance of exposure, be sure it's someone else's hand that gets caught in the till."

The British wanted to help the Romanovs, but they didn't want it known. Looking over their shoulders at their democratic allies in France and the United States, they feared further public criticism for trying to "perpetuate czarism." That was the theme of an outcry from the leftwing press in London in 1917 when word leaked out that King George V and Prime Minister Lloyd George had agreed to offer asylum to Nicholas and his family. That offer was relayed to Prince Lvov's First Provisional Government in answer to a query. For various reasons, including chaotic conditions in Russia, the message never reached the ex-Czar. Later, according to Alexander Kerensky (who succeeded Lvov as premier), the British actually refused to grant sanctuary to the Romanovs.

Importuning President Wilson to have his countrymen take charge of the long trek to Odessa most probably was the achievement of Sir William Wiseman, Chief of British Intelligence in the United States. He had swung a very similar deal the year before in persuading Wilson to put up $75,000 to help pay for "special agents" (propagandists) in Russia. Papers on this transaction are in the Public Record Office in London. The 32-year-old Wiseman, an ex-infantry officer who had been badly gassed in Flanders in 1915, had become a close friend of the 68-year-old Colonel Edward M. House, Wilson's foreign affairs mentor.

For the last years of the war Wiseman had moved into House's apartment building at 115 E. 53rd St., New York, where there were direct telephone lines to the White House and State Department. A pertinent Wiseman sentence in that June, 1917, correspondence with Sir Eric Drummond, in the Foreign Office, London, is: "You may be sure that great discretion will be used and that H.M. Government will not even unofficially appear."

There in a single sentence is that precious hallmark of traceless manipulation, of invisible nudging, which for so many years has enabled the paw-prints of the British Lion to defy the hunter's eye and the historian's reading glasses.

A hundred things could have gone wrong on that long overland trip to Odessa. Whitehall must have reasoned that if it were caught in the role of the Romanovs' guardian angel there would be hell to pay in many directions. Not so, however, if the Americans were caught. They would be saved by their reputation as pure humanitarians. And certainly no one would suspect President Wilson of aspiring to annex the Ukraine as his 49th state.

There was also an inducement in 1918 for Wilson to help the Romanovs which didn't prevail the year before. His "Fourteen Points" formula for peace already was the talk of world capitals. So was his dream of the League of Nations. The British, with French backing, were toying with the notion of settling the pesky Russian problem by holding a conference of Red and White leaders somewhere outside of Russia. This conference was later scheduled to take place on the Turkish island of Prinkipo, in the Sea of Marmora, near Constantinople.

All these auguries made it easier and easier for Wilson to picture his part in the postwar turmoil as the grand arbiter of international justice. Within such a format a Czar on ice, so to speak, ready to be led out of his sepulchre at the psychological moment, could have a good effect on the wound-healing processes in his country; especially if, this time, he offered himself or his son as a constitutional monarch, a figurehead to rally around. (The Prinkipo Conference almost, but not quite, came off. The Reds accepted, but the Whites ultimately declined to appear.)

The conclusive mark of Whitehall's involvement comes at the end. At Odessa the British made off with the prize — the seven Romanovs — and never told the world what they did with their royal cargo then or since.

No matter where the Romanovs proceeded immediately after leaving Odessa, where did they finally settle?

Pending the advent of more facts, it is the Polish Connection that is supported by the largest amount of corroboration. According to Colonel Goleniewski, the seven Romanovs converged in Warsaw in late 1919. Their sponsor, he said, was Marshal Jozef Pilsudski, the George Washington of modern Poland, a man who had served two stretches in Czarist jails. After a while, said Goleniewski, the seven divided into the four-two-one pattern already described. Nicholas, Alexandra, Marie and Alexei moved into the countryside. Olga and Tatiana went to Germany. Anastasia came to the United States.

By this version Alexandra died in 1924 in Poland, but Nicholas lived to the age of 84. He passed away on May 18, 1952, in the tiny Polish village of Ciosaniec and was buried six miles outside the town in the cemetery of Wolsztyn under his assumed name, "Michal Goleniewski." If this lifespan of the former Czar of All the Russias is accurate, it should not be overlooked that he could have sired one, two or three other children and that Colonel Goleniewski himself could be one of them.

At first it strikes a casual reader as rather implausible that an anti-Czarist like Pilsudski would take up with Nicholas, even in the underground, and even if both were strongly anti-Bolshevik. But a ray of light may have been cast unwittingly on the situation by Robin Bruce Lockhart in his biography of British Agent Sidney Reilly entitled *Ace of Spies.*

The possible mixer of this strange amalgam was no less a personage than Winston Churchill. He was then War and Air Minister of Britain and was almost alone in Lloyd George's cabinet as being in favor of backing the Russian Whites with arms, money, troops and secret agents. (Russia's Red versus White campaigns were known in Britain as "Winston's War.") Lockhart tells in his book how Churchill fell under the spell of Boris Savinkoff, War Minister under Kerensky and an eloquent Russian who could match Churchill drink for drink and story for story, far into the night. According to Lockhart, Churchill sent Savinkoff, whom he called "second to none in ruthlessness," to Warsaw along with British agents Sidney Reilly and Paul Dukes to work with Pilsudski in stirring up rebellion against the Reds in South Russia. A beardless Nicholas in the underground, wearing the uniform of a Polish Army officer and rallying Poles and Russians alike against the hated Reds, would have fitted superbly into this Churchillian picture.

A surprising clue to the fact that Winston Churchill must have had personal knowledge of the survival of the Imperial family lies in *The Great War,* Churchill's massive history of World War I. This work, comprising almost 1700 pages, devotes several chapters to Russia, including Chapter 65, "The Russian Collapse," Chapter 82, "Russia Forlorn," Chapter 83, "Intervention," and Chapter 90, "The Russian Civil War," which together describe in depth the Russian struggles from 1917 through 1919. Churchill was a careful and accurate historian. Nearly all of Chapter 65 is concerned with the abdication of Nicholas II and the ruin of the Russian armies; many pages are given to the Revolution, to the Treaty of Brest-Litovsk, and to such events as the fall and execution of Admiral Alexandr Kolchak, Commander-in-Chief of the White Russian forces.

Yet nowhere in his history does Churchill say that the Imperial family was executed! Only once in the entire work is the execution mentioned — in a caption under a photograph of the cellar at Ipatiev House. The writing style in all the captions is quite different from that of Churchill, indicating that they were added later by the photo editor. At the opening of Chapter 83, referring to the date of December 2, 1917, Churchill writes: "The Czar had abdicated and was already approaching the slaughterhouse of Ekaterinburg." *This is Mr. Churchill's last and final settlement about Czar Nicholas II. He does not tell us the Czar arrived; that he was slaughtered in the"slaughterhouse," or any other word of his fate.* One can only conclude that Churchill omitted such a momentous and barbaric event as the murder of Nicholas, Alexandra, and their children from his otherwise detailed history because he was forced to choose between remaining silent or falsifying his facts — and he chose the first course, taking the truth with him to his grave.

One question raised by readers of the Chivers Papers is how, physically, such detailed wireless messages could be transmitted from the heart of war-torn Russia to Washington, D.C., halfway around the world? Only eleven years before the outbreak of World War I, Guglielmo Marconi's great invention had spanned the Atlantic when, on January 19, 1903, the United States and England were linked by a wireless exchange of greetings between President Theodore Roosevelt and King Edward VII. By 1912 many ocean-going vessels had their own spark-station wireless units, but small, portable transmitters and receivers were still many years away.

World War I stimulated great pioneering in the field of long distance wireless. In 1918 the U.S. Army built its Lafayette Station at Crois d'Hins, near Bordeaux, for transatlantic messages. The equipment was more than double the strength of any predecessor and gained worldwide ranges with a wave length greater than

20,000 meters. Somewhat smaller units were installed at St. Assise, near Paris, and Nauen (after the German surrender) near Berlin. But in the years preceding 1914, and for most of the war, communications of the foreign embassies in Russia usually went via the national cable and telegraph system which was operated by the postal department. Nations were loath to risk their sensitive coded messages to the wireless; eavesdropping was too easy, and the heavier the traffic, the better the chance to decipher the code. Cryptology as it is now known was not very far advanced. Therefore both embassies and military commands preferred to confine their coded dispatches to telegraph and cable, where only a few persons eyed the message and there was a minimum opportunity for interception by second, third and fourth parties.

U.S. diplomats in the Russia of World War I used three cipher systems, the Green Code, the Red Code and the Mixed-Blue Code. To the best of the recollection of some persons still alive, the Green Code was considered the most complicated and secure.

Between 1914 and 1919 the U.S. Embassy in Russia twice changed its site. During those five years, and from three different locations, it used the Russian telegraph and cable network except for a modest period of time when the U.S. Consulate General in Moscow was allowed to activate a new wireless set that reached Paris. This was the general rule during the three stages in which America was first a neutral while the Czarist regime was at war from 1914 to 1917; then a wartime ally of the Provisional Government until late 1917, and last a neutral again after the Bolshevik takeover from late 1917 onward. During these fluctuations our embassy moved with the rest of the foreign diplomatic corps from Petrograd (St. Petersburg) to Vologda, then from Vologda to Archangel. About the time Lenin switched his capital from Petrograd to Moscow in midwinter of 1917–18, the U.S. Consulate General in Moscow acquired new wireless equipment and more skilled operators and set up a lively traffic in both coded and uncoded messages with American stations in England and France. It wasn't long before this Consulate General's wireless began to stick in the Bolsheviks' craw. They ordered it shut down in the Spring of 1918. This left the United States, along with most of the other foreign countries, unable to communicate with their Russian-sited diplomats and armed services attachés in any way, except by courier, that couldn't be screened by the host country. Vigorous protests about this, but to little avail, were filed almost weekly with Lenin's government by the various foreign ambassadors.

That is a sketchy outline of the facilities available to the sender, or senders, of the Chivers messages. An interesting sidelight of the new Bolshevik Government's wireless capabilities can be found in the chronicles of the first and second diplomatic gatherings at Brest- Litovsk in late 1917 and early 1918. Historians note that both Lenin and Trotsky used the Czar's relatively new wireless equipment at Tsarskoe Selo to communicate with the Germans on matters pertaining to the Brest-Litovsk armistice, dates of assembly, terms, second conference, etc. The Germans didn't like it. They complained that wireless messages offered no way of authenticating the signature of the sender. They asked that a courier be entrusted with each message duly signed and validated. It is unclear to what extent the Russians complied.

I was fortunate in obtaining a firsthand account of those 1918 and 1919 communications problems from two Americans who were on the scene. Both are still alive and in good health. Both were attached to the U.S. Embassy in Russia. Both live in New York. Both left Russia to enjoy distinguished diplomatic careers spanning more than two generations. They are Norman Armour, now eighty-seven, who served as our ambassador to several countries, including Spain and Argentina, before retiring in 1946, and who, after his retirement, was twice recalled for special missions, once by President Truman, once by President Eisenhower; and Earl L. Packer, who is now eighty.

Mr. Armour is a handsome six-footer whose courtly manners and parliamentary diction would befit a Conservative British prime minister with a warm sense of humor. In sharp contrast, Mr. Packer is a slim, bright-eyed bantam of 145 pounds, five-feet-seven, with a literary bent. The two are close friends. Both were very junior representatives of the U.S. in the Russia of World War I. Mr. Armour started out as third secretary of the embassy and rose to be second secretary. Mr. Packer, seven years younger, began his career as a minor embassy clerk but was recruited into the U.S. Army when our military mission arrived in Russia too late to save Kerensky's Government as a fighting ally in 1917.

Thereafter, as an Army lieutenant, Mr. Packer served as an assistant military attaché (but transferred back to the Foreign Service after the war). Both he and Mr. Armour remained with U.S. Ambassador David R. Francis as the embassy shuttled to Vologda and Archangel. Mr. Armour saw Admiral McCully frequently and remembers him as "a highly efficient officer of great character." Mr. Packer not only saw a great deal of Admiral McCully but vividly recalls the Admiral's two Naval Intelligence aides: Sergius Riis, whom he met at Vologda, and Hugo William Koehler, whom he encountered in Europe after the war.

"As the young Third Secretary," said Mr. Armour, "I was often stuck in the evening with the job of encoding and sending the ambassador's messages. It took a lot of time. Everything in the matter of dispatches seemed to happen at night when the code clerk was off duty. During the first months of my assignment, Ambassador Francis felt that his advice was needed in Washington on all kinds of subjects and he would send very long messages which kept me in the code room for hours. I remember once working there with an associate on an especially long dispatch from the ambassador which at last ended in the three words 'still snowing here.'

" 'Lord!' exclaimed my associate, 'that certainly must be the most expensive weather report ever sent anywhere by anyone!'

"Actually, it was a very good report. I had the highest regard for Ambassador Francis."

All these dispatches were taken to the post office for telegraph and cable transmission, Mr. Armour said. That was the standard operating procedure in Petrograd, Vologda or Archangel, except for the short period when the Consulate General in Moscow was allowed to use its wireless. But after the embassy reached Archangel the telegraph was cut in the early summer of 1918 by the formation of a fighting front between the Whites and the Reds along the railroad line leading up from the south.

Then the embassy had to rely on couriers like Assistant Military Attaché E. Francis Riggs and the signal equipment of the U.S.

Naval vessels at Archangel under Admiral McCully's command. For a while, until the Bolsheviks silenced the American wireless in Moscow, couriers took the dispatches down from the north and turned them over to Consul General DeWitt Clinton Poole for relay to Paris. On the other hand, even under Lenin's regime, the Russian telegraph and cable system kept on functioning, though Mr. Armour believes that in 1918 most of its overseas traffic was routed through Vladivostok, perhaps as a result of cables being cut in the waters to the west.

Mr. Packer recounted: "There was a great deal of diplomatic courier traffic on the railroad from Vologda to Moscow as the Bolsheviks began their crackdown on foreigners in 1918.

"Even junior officers like myself became involved. Norman Armour may not remember it, but it was he who suggested that I go to Moscow with a coded dispatch that came in one day and proved to be impossible for us to decipher. He thought someone in Moscow at the Consulate General might be able to decode it. So off I went with it to Moscow. (The trip over a meandering railroad right-of-way was close to 400 miles).

"I also remember that the military men in the embassy used an Army code and the Naval men used a Navy code. Their messages had to be deciphered by the War or Navy Departments before they were passed along — if they were important enough to be passed — to the State Department or the President."

Amid all the obstacles and confusion, however, there remained one advantage for the dispatch of the Chivers messages. All the evidence indicates that the domestic telegraph system, from the Baltic to the Black Sea, from the Western borders of Russia to the Pacific, remained operable except in the rare instances when the Reds and Whites decided to disrupt the lines for military reasons. Their reluctance to do so throughout the Red-White War is interesting. It may be traceable to a desire on both sides to listen in on the other. Or to a desire in fluid and fast-moving hostilities to keep the lines in shape for the victor's use. It is notable that even though Sverdlov's special agent, Vasily Yakovlev, found himself blocked by hostile district soviets in Omsk and Ekaterinburg after he came to get the Romanovs in Tobolsk in the Spring of 1918, he and his private telegrapher had no trouble exchanging messages with Moscow. Doubtless dozens of operators along the way, both Red and White in their leanings, were doing their best to unscramble what the whispering wires were saying — in code.

Let's apply some of this basic information to the realities confronting the Chivers agents. The messages themselves tell us that Kiyaki (Kuroki) was as worried as their sender or senders about their safe delivery and freedom from interception. We read, from the message of September 14, 1918: "Daily it is more difficult to be sure these wireless codes are sent to you. The chief of staff is most correct and careful and doesn't dispatch papers unless he is sure they complete their journey. But the territory around us is changing hands, and if towns are governed by a Soviet loyal to the government at Moscow it doesn't mean that even the nearest village is loyal also. Journeys are filled with these hazards and at all times it is my fear the wirelesses will be captured before they can be sent. So do not ask for more please. I send all I can."

The preceding paragraph is pregnant with clues. One is that the Japanese hideout had no wireless of its own and sent the messages somewhere by courier. Another is that Kiyaki handled the message problem and decided when and how the outgoing dispatches should be routed. Another is that the sender faced the fact that Kiyaki might read what he had written, coded or not, and therefore he had best be very politic in what he stated about the Nipponese chief of staff. (This he was — in spades!) Yet another, as mentioned before, is that Kiyaki was as worried as the sender or senders of the Chivers messages about the prospects of their being seized or intercepted.

Reference to the nearby territory "changing hands" applied to Ekaterinburg. That principal city of the Ural District Soviet had a telegraph office, and in the long stretch from mid-July to mid-December a well-guarded courier could have taken the Chivers dispatches from the Japanese hideout for transmission from Ekaterinburg. Furthermore, there were six consulates in Ekaterinburg, including the American, British and German (the last closed after the outbreak of the war). Three of them belonged to neutral countries, and though none are believed to have had their own wireless installations, it is just possible that one or two of them did. It would have been in the hoariest Japanese tradition to have acquired a working partnership with someone in one of the consulates (the Japanese were fond of working with the Italians on some matters) to take care of their dispatch traffic, either by wireless or courier. Kiyaki also could have decided to turn over the U.S.-bound messages to Henry Palmer, the American vice-consul there. Or they could have been routed to Admiral McCully in the Murmansk-Archangel area; they could have been directed to the U.S. Consulate General in Moscow; they could have been cabled to the Navy Department in Washington by way of Vladivostok. Or, perhaps, they could have been written in Russian, though encoded, to facilitate handling by Russian telegraphers, by Sergius Riis, who was fluent in the language, and addressed to the Navy in Washington.

Another possibility is that they could have been sent to the American Consulate General in Moscow for wireless to Paris in order to enjoy certain safeguards against exposure of the Romanov's hideaway. Just as wireless risked interception by eavesdroppers, it offered certain advantages over telegraph and cable against those trying to backtrack on a message to determine where it originated. Telegraphs and cables were a cinch to trace. They bore their own datelines. But wireless messages were not so easy. Pinpointing their source required time and triangulation instruments, which were not readily available in 1918. This is one angle that gives substance to the theory that, just to add a touch of insurance, the Chivers dispatches — on the way to their destination —were deliberately sent part way by wireless.

After the heavily-disguised party started on the long trip to Odessa in mid-December, the message-sending problem must have become more complicated, but by no means insuperable. There were bivouacs on the outskirts of cities and towns, many of which were on the network of Russian telegraph stations. Considering that there were Red agents in the escort, it would have been little more of a problem to file a dispatch in any of them than it was in Ekaterinburg. By and large, though, the in-transit messages are more laconic than those from Kiyaki's compound. Here the author of the reports seems to have stepped out of the shadow of Kiyaki's seniority, for though the Japanese tagged along for most of the trip, they faded away on the approaches to Odessa. (". . . our Asian friends left us at the post before the crossing into this safer territory.") And when he at last arrived in Odessa, the relief he expressed in his last message — February 17, 1919 — must have been enhanced by the assurance that the dispatch would reach Washington in a hurry. A French general headed the Allied command in the big seaport. There were U.S. destroyers in the harbor. There were dozens of other American naval vessels scattered from Constantinople, Corfu and Malta to the Western Mediterranean citadel of Gibraltar. There were wireless sets galore.

Some who have read the Chivers dispatches carefully question their authenticity because they doubt that an agent would take precious message space to report so many gossipy details about the Romanovs. This objection has merit. In some of his reports, the sender becomes as chatty and descriptive as the Marquise de Sévigné in any of her classic letters to her daughter, Françoise Marguérite. On the other hand, there is evidence that he had been instructed to supply just such revealing accounts of the morale and changing moods of his imperial charges. In his September 14, 1918 message, for example, he seems to be apologizing for the paucity of his information in two sentences: "So do not ask for more please. I send all I can."

Then again, from the September 22, 1918 message comes evidence that his superiors had found his reports so inadequate in regard to the Romanovs' condition and attitude that they sent three "American agents" to visit the compound, stay in the servants' quarters, and try to eavesdrop on the intimate conversation of Nicholas and Alexandra. Obviously the masterminds of the Chivers operation wanted much more of a fill-in than they were getting on the states of mind of Nicholas and his family, and as to whether there might be any unpleasant surprises for those who were helping them. In that context, then, and from their viewpoint, perhaps the message sender had been providing fewer details than he had been directed to.

Others find in the Chivers dispatches certain stilted phrases of

English that don't smack of American authorship. This is true. It has been pointed out elsewhere in the book that Sergius Riis — if he was one of the message senders — was more at ease in Russian than in English; that Hugo Koehler — if he was one of the senders — though thoroughly familiar with English, was disposed to use it on occasions in a flowery, continental style.

Two possibilities cannot be excluded from speculation about ways and means by which the dispatches were sent. One is that they were delivered somewhere on Russian soil to a courier plane. Several chroniclers of the Romanovs' last days before their disappearance tell how an airplane appeared one day over Ekaterinburg. It was not seen to land and no details were given about its size, mission or nationality. But the fact that a plane was around has a broad base of corroboration.

The other possibility is that the coded messages were sent to Sverdlov in Moscow and redistributed by him to the ultimate addressees. It is not unreasonable to suppose that such an arrangement had been worked out by which the highest administrative authority in Bolshevik Russia had agreed to keep all interested parties up-to-date on one of the most sensitive and intricate of operations. Its planning and execution had come from such secret collaboration. Why wouldn't the mechanics of communication — so vital to its ultimate success — have been made an integral part?

The absence of clues in the messages to the matter of how they were sent can be attributed to fear of interception. There is nothing in them to give that secret away. There is also very little in them to betray the most interesting secret of all: namely, the chain-of-command in the whole operation.

Kiyaki was "chief of staff" for the Ekaterinburg phase. A good candidate for the role of senior American in Russia on the planning and execution of "Chivers" was Newton A. McCully, the man whose acquaintance with President Wilson dated from the days when McCully was skipper of the *Mayflower;* the man whose acquaintance with the Czarist Court dated from the Russo-Japanese War, and later (1914 to 1917) when he was U.S. Naval Attaché in St. Petersburg.

But who was in overall control of "Chivers" from the time it was dreamed up and pieced together to the time it was finished and almost all traces of it destroyed? Was he a Briton, a Red, a White, an American, a Japanese, a German, a Cossack, or perhaps a neutral Swiss or Swede?

It is one of the most interesting mysteries left unresolved. If there are any clues to the answer in the Chivers dispatches, I have missed them. And if there *is* a clue in them, it should be regarded as a flaw in the otherwise faultless planning which clearly intended that the clue shouldn't be there.

Who was Kiyaki?

PART III

THE RESCUERS

The Escape of Czar Nicholas and Alexandra

PETER BESSELL

*Peter Bessell served as a Liberal Party member of
Parliament from 1964-66 and 1966-70.*

I AM SATISFIED beyond any reasonable doubt that the Russian Imperial Family, i.e., the last Czar, Nicholas II, his wife and children, were not, as has long been supposed, assassinated at Ekaterinburg in July 1918, or, for that matter, elsewhere at any other time. With the carefully camouflaged assistance of two or more of the then Allied governments, and the collaboration of the Russian government, they escaped to a country of relative safety, where they lived under assumed names.

The evidence for this exists in the files of several Western governments and it is time for it to be published. For reasons which I will explain, I accept that the policy which was adopted by the governments of those countries was inevitable in

1918 and in the years that followed. Today, I cannot accept that any valid political reason exists which supersedes the obligation of present governments to the accuracy of history. The increasing mountain of evidence of the escape and the total destruction of the alleged evidence of the assassination will inevitably lead to an eventual unofficial disclosure of the facts. In these circumstances, I believe that the governments of the major Western powers, as well as the Soviet Union, should declassify the relevant papers and jointly, or separately, make a public statement for the benefit of historians and students of Imperial Russia and the immediate post-revolutionary period.

It is notable that the Soviet Union has been pre-

The headline and opening paragraphs of Peter Bessell's article in the June, 1971 issue of *East Europe* magazine. This was written after he had learned in London that there was a secret codicil to the Brest-Litovsk Treaty of March 3, 1918 in which the Bolshevik Government agreed to the German demand that "the Imperial Family of Russia" be granted "safe passage" out of the country.

CHAPTER 11

THE JAPANESE

Of all the foreign espionage organizations in the Russia of World War I, the Imperial Japanese Secret Service allowed the least to be known about it. That in itself may be a tribute to its skill. It may also be a sign of its modest scope of operations (at that time) in Western cities. The Mikado's men had the reputation for playing all their cards in the realm of secret intelligence-gathering well out of view of Western eyes, whether or not those eyes were Allied or hostile. Considering the part played by Emperor Yoshihito's stewards in the Romanovs' rescue, there can be little doubt that they were far more proficient than was generally believed at the time. That, too, was a prime asset in the success of Chivers. In the long hiding of the Imperial Family not very far from Ekaterinburg, near the hamlets of Koptyaka and Bizim-Baievsk, the Japanese provided the touch of "what you'd least suspect," which was echoed all over again by the Americans when they shepherded the fugitives on the long traverse from the Urals to Odessa.

Many influences were behind the Nipponese disinclination to talk to the Allies about their secrets. In the first place, the collapse of Czarist Russia had already triggered long-range Japanese plans to take over the Maritime Provinces and other chunks of Eastern Siberia, but the time had not come, in the first months of 1918, to make the fact known. In the second place, distrust of all foreigners permeated the Samurai caste whose concepts dominated the thinking of the empire's marshals and admirals. Though the shogunate — the hereditary supreme command of the Army — had been abolished in 1867, the notion of the command's freedom from all but imperial restraints lingered in the two advisory bodies to the Emperor: the Gensuifu, comprised entirely of marshals and fleet admirals, and the Gunji Sangiin, or military council. That included generals, admirals, war minister, naval minister and chiefs of the general and service staffs. The term "advisory bodies" was a purified form of the truth. Actually they were wardens and watchdogs. The Emperor was more their prisoner than their ruler on military policy. For that reason it is believed — but not known for certain — that the Imperial Japanese Secret Service was manned, staffed, trained and directed under the joint supervision of the Gensuifu and Gunjo Sangiin. Through this system, and with the help of IJSS, the brass hats were able to perpetuate the very convenient tradition of being responsible only to the throne and not being answerable to either Parliament or the public. Since the throne was really under their thumb, so to speak, on matters of greatest importance to them, they were actually answerable to no one. They had it made. But they had every reason in the world not to want to advertise the fact.

Another factor which made Japanese espionage activities more opaque than most, was the simple truth that no Nipponese found it easy to masquerade as a Westerner or blend into the scenery of Western capitals. For especially sensitive missions abroad, outsiders had to be hired. Often they were Caucasians with a proved record of dissent against the target government. But as contract agents they had to be distrusted for the very reason that they were non-Japanese. Therefore they were not told more than was absolutely necessary. They were handled as pieceworkers. Sometimes they were deliberately misled.

It was quite typical of the Japanese that their outpost in the Ural District of Siberia was not in the city of Ekaterinburg but fifteen miles to the northwest. They called it a trading post. It was truly a listening post. In Ekaterinburg they would have been subject to intensive scrutiny by foreigners. Their comings and goings could have been kept under surveillance by consular officials of several nations. Their senior officers would have been expected to merge into the clubby atmosphere exuded by such diplomats as Sir Thomas Preston, the Britisher, and his consular colleagues from six other countries. The rounds of dinners, teas and luncheons, with the smalltalk and rumormongering, would have been inescapable.

But not if one is fifteen miles out of town. There one is out of range of most of the socializing, the doorbell ringing, the eavesdropping, the peeping through curtain windows.

So there the Japanese maintained themselves in a walled compound. By the summer of 1918 it was protected by an infantry detachment. It was an ideal hideout for fugitives. And it was a site from which it was easy enough to send a junior officer to one of those social gatherings in Ekaterinburg, from time to time, to find out what the latest rumors were.

None of those planning "Chivers," including the Japanese, had any way of knowing, of course, that the very month the Romanovs would be sprung from their captors was going to be one of the bloodiest in the Russian Revolution — July, 1918. On July 6 the new German Ambassador, Count Wilhelm Mirbach, was assassinated in a Social-Revolutionary plot in which our old friend Vasily Yakovlev may have taken some part. It was a signal for an uprising of Left Social Revolutionaries in Moscow. That same evening the Cheka acted to forestall the assassination of Bolshevik leaders in the Moscow Opera House. The whole chain of events incited a crackdown by the Cheka in cities all over the country. It was a terror campaign which lasted for weeks and evolved into so many raids and shootings that many Allied agents including Sidney Reilly (for a while) had to flee into the hinterland or leave Russia. This was the purge that raided and ruined Colonel de Vertement's French intelligence organization and brought the banishment of the famed spymaster, X. B. Kalamatiano, an American of Greek descent and Byzantine connections. As the month wore on, the Cheka drive was rendered grimmer than ever by White uprisings in several cities which turned out to be ill-timed and prematurely staged to synchronize with the Anglo-American landing in Archangel in August. (This had been delayed, but notice of the delay hadn't filtered to all the Whites.)

It is hard to believe that the Japanese weathered all these storms with the vanished Romanovs in their custody. Very obviously they were well battened down in their "refuge surrounded by walls and gardens with but two gateways, each with a guardhouse." By reading between the lines of the Chivers messages, a minimal number of Russians, if any, were allowed through the two gateways. The Japanese apparently didn't rely on Russian servants for anything. Cooking, baking, laundering and housecleaning chores must have been done by members of the infantry company. The hideaway was a model of self-containment.

The Japanese Foreign Ministry was asked a few months ago for biographical material on Colonel Kiyaki as well as for its official version of what happened to the Romanovs. Over a period of time the questions were fenced off with exquisite courtesy and consummate unhelpfulness. In respect to Colonel Kiyaki, a spokesman finally said there was "nothing on him." In respect to the Romanovs, the answer was precisely the same as that given to the BBC at about the same time, namely: "The Ministry of Foreign Affairs is not in a position to answer your questions. We hope you will understand."

Histories and memoirs written about the Japanese incursions in Asia at that time mention no one by the name of Kiyaki. It could have been a cover name. There are many references, however, to two high-powered Japanese operatives in Siberia — Shinkei Kuroki and his son, Shinkei, Junior. They enjoyed honorary titles as Colonel and Captain, respectively.

The elder Kuroki was a nephew of a great national hero, General Tamesada Kuroki, who distinguished himself in the Chino-Japanese War of 1894–95 and in the Russo-Japanese War of 1904–05.

He was created baron for his services in the former war, and count for his leadership of the First Army in the latter. He was a potent member of the Imperial Military Establishment. There is a potential phonetic resemblance between "Kiyaki" and "Kuroki;" especially if one or the other of the words was spoken by a Nipponese into the ears of an American who could have misunderstood the syllables as the Japanese chief of staff introduced himself.

There's no question that the Kurokis were influential in the Japanese operations in Siberia. Starting as early as January, 1918 the elder Kuroki served as a kind of roving ambassador between the White Russians and the Japanese military and for several months remained at the headquarters of General Grigory Semenov, Ataman of the Trans-Baikal Cossacks. Both Kurokis bob up in a number of historical studies, including one by a Columbia professor who had access to Japanese archives, *The Japanese Thrust in Siberia*, by James Morley.

Publication of the Chivers Papers may render the figure of Colonel Kiyaki (or Colonel Kuroki) one of the most famous in Russo-Japanese relations. It was he who embodied Emperor Yoshihito's abiding interest in seeing that the Romanovs were shepherded to safety. It was he who represented the Mikado's down payment of $75,000 in the venture. It was he who had to snatch the prisoners with the help of other agents from Ipatiev House in the middle of the night of July 16/17, and hide, house and feed them for many restless weeks. It was he who had to provide protection against interlopers, cope with the Romanovs' complaints and peccadilloes, dicker with agents of other nations and help iron out details of the long trip to Odessa, probably aided by Admiral Newton A. McCully and General John J. Pershing.

Kiyaki's story would make a fine book. Let us hope someone in Tokyo — perhaps in the secret service, the Army, the Foreign Ministry or the palace — can find enough data to put it together. It could reflect nothing but honor on the royal house of Japan.

Disclosure of the American, British and Bulgarian versions may be enough to shake loose the Japanese Version, and so add a fourth interpretation by foreigners of what happened to the Romanovs.

By that time the Kremlin may be shamed into offering its own story, though that is probably only a wild dream. The Kremlin is rarely shamed into anything. The sorrowful truth is that both the United States and Britain have played their possession of the Romanov papers in the Kremlin's own style. For more than fifty-six years they both denied knowing anything about a Romanov rescue. It took ten years of pressure by a great many persons to throw any light on it at all.

CHAPTER 12

THE BRITISH

There are many reasons why revolution-torn Russia was the place where Britain's Secret Intelligence Service (SIS) assigned agents on what was probably the largest scale in its history. The size and resources of the British Empire at that time were immense. This meant that trained agents were available from outposts all over the world and there was no lack of money to pay them. The amount of Russian territory that had to be covered — more than one-seventh of the world's land surface — ranked somewhere near the size of the British Empire itself. SIS men had to be sent to such widely-separated cities as Archangel, Vladivostok, Kiev, Odessa, Murmansk and all the major stops on the Trans-Siberian Railway.

The Russian political factions that constantly threatened to become dominant overnight or the day after tomorrow were numerous and infinitely complex. Some kind of contact had to be maintained with the old Liberals, the Mensheviks, the Social Revolutionaries, the Cossacks, the boyars, the Navy, the Czarists and the Northern, Southern and Eastern generals. As for the Bolsheviks and the jockeying White groups, each were multicolored coalitions of power and personalities requiring close cultivation by different SIS agents whose job it was to make each believe that it enjoyed the secret backing of certain British leaders, and that if it ultimately gained ascendancy the secret backing might become official. Great dollops of hope and cash were the SIS's stock in trade.

Then, too, there were signs that the whole enormous Russian state was coming apart and that its breakup would offer Western nations remarkable opportunities for acquiring land, mineral wealth, trading concessions and spheres of influence. Britain had dreamed of such a sphere of influence in the Baltic. The Admiralty, in fact, had cast an eye towards the possibility of extending its domination of the Mediterranean into the Black Sea and land-locked Caspian. The French and Italians coveted sectors of South Russia and, of course, the Japanese could hardly wait to get their hands on the Maritime Provinces.

Finally, it was an era of unsettlement and grandiose scheming in which the stakes were apt to go to the nation that was as well equipped in the espionage field as she was in military or naval power. Britain was just such a nation. It was a day for foxes as well as lions. So the foxes of Britain were let loose to run all over the former lands of the Czar. SIS probably had more trained manpower on the scene than all the other Western powers combined, though the others, including the United States, were racing to catch up. The situation was ready-made for one SIS triumph after another.

Hindsight tells us that, with all these latent advantages, Britain would have profited more substantially in the early years of the Bolshevik regime if the pervasive chicanery of her SIS men hadn't frightened Lenin's Government into fashioning a secret police organization, the Cheka, whose ruthless qualities made it infamous throughout the world; and if the British Government, under a succession of prime ministers, had been able to make up its mind how to deal with the Bolsheviks while there was any trust whatsoever left between them.

But the fumbling in London should not obscure the fact that inside the upheaving Russia of those days, SIS had one of the most extensive corps of spies ever maintained by one nation within the borders of another. In it were men reflecting all degrees of derring-do, military experience, culture, breeding, subtlety and political outlook. It had rough diamonds and polished con men. It had someone for everyone.

It had men like that famous and brilliant bounder, Sidney Reilly, the master of disguise. He was said to have eleven different passports and a "wife" to go with each. Among his credentials were those identifying him as an official of the Cheka. Reilly came close to witnessing the success of his plot to have all key members of the Bolshevik hierarchy murdered, but the Social Revolutionaries jumped the gun on him and advanced the date to a meeting in the Moscow Opera House on the night of July 6, 1918. That was less than two weeks before the Romanovs were rescued from Ipatiev House. The Bolshevik leaders were saved when a left-leaning French newspaperman, René Marchand, (whom the French intelligence chief in Russia, Colonel de Vertement, had taken into his confidence), tipped off the Cheka to the plot. Reilly was equally skilled in poisoning, shooting, stabbing or throttling his adversaries. He was one of the three SIS agents sent to Warsaw after the end of the Red-White war.

It had men like the athletic naval aviator, William Peer-Groves, a former RAF major. He liked to wear a kimono and melt into the Oriental scenery. He was a practitioner of jiu-jitsu. He had lived in Japan for years. When he wasn't busy on his SIS assignments he attended to his personal obligations as a disciple of the Mahayana School of Zen Buddhism, and he was so courtly and charming that after his services to the fugitive Imperial Family, whatever they were (and they probably included the task of escorting them on their journey from Odessa, for he was stationed in South Russia at the time), the SIS sent him to make a personal report to Nicholas's mother when she arrived in Malta. His name appears on the visitors' list of the Dowager Empress Marie at the San Antonio Palace under the date of April 23, 1919. Tony Summers of BBC recently traced Peer-Groves's daughter, Mrs. Catherine Clarkson, to a country home in Cornwall. She said her father had told her of the rescue of the Imperial Family of Russia but, as she recalled, reported that

Nicholas himself had lost his life. If that's what he told her, it is believed he was simply living up to his commitment with the Official Secrets Act never to disclose that the last Czar had survived.

It had men like Bruce Lockhart, the urbane and literary diplomatist. He had the cover rank of British Consul-General. He became especially close to Trotsky. It was through Trotsky that he was able to pass on an invitation for a British naval mission to come over and reorganize the Red Navy, and for a British transportation expert to run the Soviet railways. London turned down both bids. Lockhart was one of the few Britons to predict that the Bolsheviks would remain in power for years and that the dreams of the Whites and the Czarists were hopeless. As time confirmed his evaluations of chaotic conditions, the intelligence reports that he smuggled out later assumed the status of classics in both the SIS and the Foreign Office.

Other colorful and versatile characters on the SIS roster were:

Paul Dukes (later Sir Paul), who posed successfully in Russia as a cringing epileptic, a bearded peasant, a pale and disgruntled intellectual, and Comrade Piotrovsky, a Communist Party committeeman. In 1915 Dukes had been made a member of the Anglo-Russian Commission and given a passport as a King's Messenger. It enabled him to carry out a roving assignment to find out what was going on among the revolutionaries all over Russia. He spoke Russian with ease, having come to the country in 1909 to study music in St. Petersburg. He had friends among the leaders of different revolutionary factions. After the Bolsheviks took over, he sank even deeper into local camouflage by joining the Communist Party and enlisting in the Red Army. Paul Dukes was one of the agents sent to Warsaw, at Winston Churchill's instigation, after the war.

There were many others of great resourcefulness — Lieutenant W. S. Agar, R.N., who won the Victoria Cross for his work in a special group of fast torpedo-patrol boats which operated a courier service for SIS agents in Russia; Captain George Hill, another buccaneering sleuth of the Sidney Reilly school; William Le Queux, SIS's "man with Kerensky"; Lt. Col. Frederick M. Bailey, master of the art of living-like-a-native, who was positioned in Russian Turkestan; Major Latham Valentine Stewart Baker, the aviator who later became the first pilot to fly over Mount Everest; Major Stephen Alley and Commander Ernest Boyce, who at various times were SIS chiefs inside Russia.

All these agents and many others were under the overall command of an old Navy man who has become a great figure in the history of British Intelligence. He was Captain Mansfield Cumming, a leader to become famous in the international game of wits simply as "C." He had been appointed the first director of MI 1c, the original designation for MI-6, when it was was set up in 1911 as an aggressive espionage agency designed to go after the plans and secrets of other nations. (MI 1c had its name changed to MI-6 some time in the 1930s, and so it remains today.) Cumming became so legendary, in fact, that his title of "C" floated over to his proud successors.

Cumming was a gay dog with a penchant for fast cars and women only a bit slower than the cars. In the early months of his regime he brought scores of new types into the service and did a great deal to make it less stuffy and pompous. He had lost a leg in an automobile accident and was fond of shocking certain stiff individuals by striking matches on his wooden leg or tapping it with a paper knife while interviewing them. He was always on the lookout for what he termed "the cut of the jib of an alert agent." He recruited only those who struck his fancy. He is credited with a psychological coup over the Germans in the years immediately preceding World War I. He secretly encouraged British judges to hand out light sentences to the few spies from the Wilhemstrasse who were arrested, in order to give Berlin a false sense of security, encourage its espionage operations, and thus enable SIS to trace more and more German agents up to the moment war was declared. The strategy succeeded very well.

The Britons already named are only a fraction of the SIS men, most working full time, but some only part time, in Revolutionary Russia. A good example of the part-timers was Robert Wilton of the *London Times*. He is the newspaperman who told the unbelieving

Joseph Lasies, on the platform of the Ekaterinburg railroad station, "Commander Lasies, even if the Czar and Imperial Family are living, it is necessary to say that they are dead."

More than half a century later, a team of reporters from the British Broadcasting Corporation were able to trace such large sums of money wired to Wilton in Russia by the Foreign Office, that BBC became convinced that Wilton was a British agent. His role over several years in assailing skeptics of the "assassination" tends to bear that out.

Of all its penetrations into the highest councils of foreign governments in the years of World War I, the British Secret Service pulled off its greatest coup, not in Russia, Europe or Asia, but in the figure of its "Man in America" — Sir William Wiseman. This thirty-year-old Cambridge graduate, with his pleasant manners and unhurried speech, worked himself into such an intimate relationship with President Wilson's principal aide and adviser — Colonel Edward M. House — that he was allowed to read virtually all the White House mail and dispatches on topics of interest to Britain. Both Wilson and House sought his advice on policies in the making. He was taken along to counsel them still further at the Paris peace negotiations. At a ripening stage of his friendship with the top Americans, he took up residence in the apartment house at 115 E. 53rd Street, New York, where House lived on the ninth floor, and where there was a private telephone to the White House and State Department.

Wiseman's post was several thousand miles west of both London and Moscow. Yet he probably had more to do with getting the Americans and British together on the rescue of the Romanovs than any other single person.

Starting as early as 1916, the British astutely routed all their urgent business with the Americans through the magic glow of rapport that shone on the Wilson-House-Wiseman level. If the subjects were vital, it made no difference what branches of the governments were involved — Foreign Office, State Department, Munitions Board, Admiralty, Navy, Supply Board, Army, War Office, Purchasing Commission, Intelligence — all the papers were first funneled through Wiseman. He was likewise consulted on many of the American papers being prepared for London. He was frequently asked to improve statements by President Wilson on matters of international policy, both before Wilson left for his first trip abroad, and later, back in the United States, before the President's second trip. He had become, in fact, a super-ambassador as well as SIS chief in the United States.

CHAPTER 13

THE AMERICANS

The identities of British SIS agents have emerged one by one over the years from scores of books and studies written about the Russian Revolution. The American names are harder to come by because much less has been put down on paper about them. It requires sophisticated guessing to choose from among the agents who were in Russia at the time those who may have worked directly on some phase of the Romanov rescue. At least thirteen Americans did; that much is gleaned from the Chivers Papers. The papers themselves were authored largely by one of those agents. The CIA undoubtedly knows who he was, but is restricted by policy as well as law from identifying him.

In starting to narrow down the list of Americans, one is faced with a wide assortment of personalities. First, there was the beefed-up staff of the American Embassy, including a number of military attachés. During 1918 numerous U.S. intelligence officers were landed in the Murmansk, Archangel and Vladivostok areas, along with two skeleton infantry regiments under the command of

Major General William S. Graves. A few of these military men wound up in the widely-scattered headquarters of White generals. One, for example, was David Prescott Barrows — later to become President of the University of California. A scholarly soldier, Barrows arrived in Russia as an intelligence officer on General Graves' staff and soon became closely associated with the Cossack Ataman, General Grigori Semonov.

From the ranks of American businessmen came another group of candidates — the far-flung personnel of the International Harvester Company in Moscow, Omsk, Novo-Nikolaievsk, Vladivostok and Ekaterinburg. Cyrus H. McCormick, the famed head of International Harvester, and a member of the Root Commission, crossed Siberia in the spring of 1917 on the former imperial train of Czar Nicholas II and gave a dinner for no fewer than thirty of his employes in Moscow's National Hotel on the evening of June 23. Mr. McCormick knew a great many influential persons in the last Czarist regime who later retained some of their prestige under Kerensky. It is possible that McCormick was the man who picked Chicago prosecutor Roy C. Woods for a secret mission to meet with Tatiana in Poland in 1923.

Among the large list of International Harvester employes in Russia was Henry L. Palmer. He served as U.S. Vice Consul at Ekaterinburg from April, 1918, to September, 1919. During this period he was handed scores of assignments by his government and it is hard to believe that Mr. Palmer wasn't in on some aspects of the rescue, if not a direct participant. It is most likely that he would have parcelled out special missions to other young Harvester men in Russia at the time, and some could still be alive.

Another source of amateur American intelligence manpower was the YMCA staff who had been working in Russia with prisoners of war. Their unit operations were suspended after the Bolshevik takeover and their services made available to the U.S. Government.

Still another source were members of the forty-man American Red Cross Commission of which the most potent personalities were the American copper multimillionaire, Colonel William Boyce Thompson, who was born and bred in Alder Gulch, Montana, and who at first favored the idea of having the Bolsheviks overthrown by factions behind Kerensky; and Major Raymond Robins, an adventuresome figure who had scraped a fortune out of the gold in the Yukon and became very close to Trotsky. Needless to say, Thompson and Robins didn't see eye to eye about U.S. policy until the very end of their association. Then Robins won Thompson over to his conviction that the Bolsheviks would endure. The change came too late to influence the State Department.

Perhaps the most comprehensive of all the American amateur spy clusters were in the three networks described in a report to Washington on July 26, 1918 — ten days after the Romanovs disappeared — by the then Acting Consul General DeWitt Clinton Poole, Jr. He was an urbane, moustachioed young diplomat with a high forehead and a short figure who at the age of thirty-three stepped into the post vacated by the death of Madden Summers on May 3. He described the composition of the new networks as (1) regular consular officers; (2) especially appointed vice-consuls of whom Henry Palmer, at Ekaterinburg, was an example; and (3) observers and special agents.

Poole was a native of Vancouver Barracks, Washington. He went to the University of Wisconsin and took the graduate course in diplomacy at Georgetown. (For six years in the 1930s he was director of the School of Public Affairs at Princeton and later an official in the Institute of Advanced Studies there.)

Poole's detailed report on the American agents, and the help, supplies and money they funneled to the Whites, was only recently unearthed by an Auburn University (Alabama) research team headed by the Ukrainian-born history professor, Dr. Oleh Pidhainy. The team has been working on 300 reels of microfilmed documents from the State Department, covering Russo-American relations from 1801 to 1929. Dr. Pidhainy and his associates found that the launching of the three U.S. espionage networks resulted from a $10 million fund at first requested by Felix Willoughby Smith, the U.S. Consul at Tiflis in Russian Georgia, a day or two after the Bolsheviks seized power in 1917. It was later approved by President Wilson. Dr. Pidhainy's findings were first made known in a lengthy article by Margaret Shannon in the magazine section of the *Journal and Constitution,* Atlanta, Ga., on Jan. 12, 1975. The importance of them emanates from their proof that the United States intervened secretly against the Bolsheviks while it claimed not to be doing so, and long before U.S. troops were landed in North Russia and Vladivostok in the summer of 1918.

All told, however, "Poole's pool of spies," as it has come to be known, was a hodge-podge of talents in which there were only a smattering of professional agents. They were mostly young businessmen, diplomats, YMCA men and Red Crossers. Of the latter, for example, the total military experience of 37 out of the 40 — all rated as Army officers from colonel down — consisted of the time required to visit a military tailor and be measured for a uniform. The correspondents in Moscow nicknamed them "the Haitian Army."

As for agents with military backgrounds, the Americans had no reason to believe that they had anything like the British array of talent in the stricken vastness of Russia, and in terms of volume they certainly didn't. In terms of quality, however, they were pleasantly surprised. There probably weren't any foreigners in Russia better equipped for secret missions by virtue of their linguistics skills, versatility and rough-and-ready outlooks than the trio who were undoubtedly involved in one or more of the stages of the Romanovs' rescue. They were Captain (later Vice Admiral) Newton A. McCully, Lieutenant (later Commander) Sergius M. Riis and Lieutenant (later Commander) Hugo William Koehler.

The oldest of the three, Newton Alexander McCully, was born in Anderson, South Carolina, on June 19, 1867. He was good in his studies at Anderson High School and at two different private schools, and was appointed to the Naval Academy by Congressman D. W. Aiken. He checked in as a plebe at Annapolis in 1883.

Annapolis first classmen didn't start publishing their class book, *Lucky Bag,* until 1894, according to a Naval Academy spokesman, so the record of McCully's undergraduate days in the class of 1887 is sparser than it is for younger men like Hugo Koehler of the class of 1909. One of McCully's adopted daughters, Mrs. John B. McDonald, has been researching this phase of his life and is writing a book on him.

"I have tried," she told me, "to find out what he was like in those days from some of the families in Anderson, as well as from other Naval officers of about the same age. They agree that he was an intense student. They say he was fond of hunting and rambling around the countryside near Anderson. Some are quite sure that he went in very hard for fencing at the Naval Academy but I never was able to pin this down."

A Naval friend of McCully's who asked not be named said that "he was not only a serious student and a deep thinker but he was customarily quite taciturn . . . close-mouthed, you might say. He preferred to let others do the talking, especially if the amenities called for small talk. But he would swing into a bull session quite vigorously if the topic interested him. Anything about the Navy or foreign affairs or history got his attention. His talk was full of historical allusions and so were the speeches that he made."

The McCully who emerged from his midshipman days was a spare figure of five-feet-nine with a black beard and moustache and dark, brooding eyes. Whatever his shortcomings might have been in social banter, he was a good listener. This probably stood in his favor years later when he became skipper of the presidential yacht *Mayflower* and hosted William Howard Taft on his Chesapeake cruises, and after him, in the early months of 1913, the even more loquacious Woodrow Wilson. His acquaintance with Wilson certainly must have had some connection with his probable assignment to the highly secret rescue of the Romanovs.

When McCully graduated from Annapolis in 1887, two years of sea duty were required by law before he and his classmates could qualify for commissions as ensign. He logged his time afloat on U.S.S. *Pensacola* and *Qinnebang*. The ensign commission finally came on July 1, 1889. Therewith began his distinguished career as a naval officer.

For the next quarter of a century McCully's assignments both at sea and ashore could hardly have been better designed to broaden his acquaintance with key statesmen, power politics, naval strategy and the gathering of intelligence. At sea he put in tours on eight ships before he was lucky enough to be on the *Bennington* when she was ordered to the Philippines to help put down the insurrection that followed the Spanish-American War. In 1901 he went to the *Oregon* for his first service on a battleship, and the following year he was posted as executive officer of U.S.S. *Dolphin*, a special dispatch ship for Secretary of the Navy John D. Long of Massachusetts. Long was a member of the Cabinets of President McKinley and President Theodore Roosevelt.

In 1907 McCully was appointed executive officer of the new armored cruiser, *California*, and remained aboard for almost three years as the vessel participated in Pacific Fleet exercises and cruised to Hawaii, Samoa, the Philippines, Japan and China.

Sandwiched between these years at sea were shoreside stretches at the Naval Ordnance Proving Ground at Indian Head, Md.; at the Naval War College in Newport; at the Torpedo School in Newport, and as Assistant Naval Attaché in St. Petersburg, Russia, which led to his designation as U.S. Observer in the Russo-Japanese War.

His reports on that conflict in the months of 1904 and 1905, particularly on the siege of Port Arthur and the Battles of Liaoyang and Mukden, attracted wide attention in the higher echelons of the Navy and War Departments and tapped him for a special assignment in the Office of Naval Intelligence from October 1905 to June 1906. It should not be forgotten that the diplomacy of President Roosevelt was largely instrumental in ending the Russo-Japanese War in the Treaty of Portsmouth which was signed on Aug. 23, 1905. McCully's expertise on that war, and on conditions in Czarist Russia, came in very handy in Washington.

When McCully was given command of the *Mayflower* in September, 1912, the Moroccan Crisis of 1911 at Agadir had already raised the specter of an imminent European War, and it is an interesting fact that no sooner had the Kaiser's armies invaded Belgium than the Navy decided to interrupt McCully's brief tour as skipper of the *California* and send him back to St. Petersburg in October, 1914. This time his appointment was Naval Attaché in the American Embassy. He stayed there until July, 1917. Then he returned to Washington as the Navy's representative in connection with the visit of the Russian Commission to the United States. Thus he had been on the Russian scene as the 300-year-old rule of the Romanovs ended with the abdication of Nicholas II on March 15,

1917. But the Bolsheviks and the "assassination" were still over a year away.

Their descendants believe that the careers of McCully, Koehler and Riis crisscrossed through the Office of Naval Intelligence shortly after the outbreak of World War I in 1914. The United States was then more than two years from becoming a combatant. Our Navy was still a relatively small organization (about 70,000 men) scattered all over the Atlantic and Pacific. The hand-picked, carefully-nurtured crew of wizards in the ONI cabin was miniscule in size. Only a fraction of its total roster could have comprised men who had been in Czarist Russia long enough to learn its customs and speak the language like a native. McCully, Koehler and Riis met those specifications. All belonged to the ONI secret society. There were all the compulsions in the world to make them known to each other, though where and how they met remains a guess. There is a bare chance that Riis, more than a decade younger than McCully, met the South Carolinian when the latter was Assistant Naval Attaché in St. Petersburg in 1904, and before he shoved off on his observer assignment in the Russo-Japanese War. Riis was then a young student in the Russian capital. If they did meet, the encounter could have been little more than perfunctory. More likely it was a number of influences that brought and kept them together later: the urgencies of the war, their naval backgrounds, ONI connections, their Russian expertise, their personal courage and their enduring favorable effects on each other after they met. The circumstantial evidence is compelling that by the time of the Bolshevik Revolution in the autumn of 1917, when Lenin and Trotsky seized power from Kerensky, McCully was very familiar with the talents of Koehler and Riis and was more than ready to adopt the pair as his special agents and protégés.

The evidence is almost as good that by the time McCully was through with his mission in Washington in the summer of 1917 he had not only refreshed his acquaintance with President Wilson (begun on the *Mayflower* in 1913), but had conferred with Colonel House, Secretary of State Lansing and Sir William Wiseman, British Intelligence Chief in the United States.

Flip the scenario ahead a few months. From readily available and nonclassified sources, let's see where McCully, Riis and Koehler were spotted in March, 1918. That is the month when the second Brest-Litovsk Conference took Russia out of the war against the Central Powers and sent Vasily Yakolev to Tobolsk to try to bring the Romanovs out of Siberia.

McCully, at that time, was commander of Squadron Five of the Atlantic Fleet Patrol Force. Its zone of operations was off the coast of France. The Navy hadn't allowed such a useful hand as McCully to loll around Washington after he was finished with the Russian Commission (a Kerensky creation which the Bolshevik coup had rendered almost meaningless). McCully had been assigned to the Atlantic Fleet in October, 1917.

Riis was in British waters serving in a mine-layer squadron. He was soon to leave for Russia as an assistant naval attaché.

Koehler was "theoretically" in Queenstown, Ireland, assigned to destroyers and submarine chasers as an aide to Captain (later Rear Admiral) Arthur J. Hepburn whose headquarters were in London. Actually, at the time, Koehler could have been in Germany. Successfully impersonating a German Naval officer, Koehler made two protracted visits to the Kaiser's home grounds during World War I — the first before we entered the war, the second afterwards.

Members of Koehler's family know about these visits to wartime Germany. They are not sure when the second one ended. Rather apocryphically, the June 19, 1941 editions of the *New York Herald Tribune* state in their obituary on Commander Koehler that he "was the first American Naval officer to enter Germany after the war." They could have more truthfully stated that he was the first American Naval officer to make two visits to Germany before the Armistice in the uniform of a German Naval officer.

By June, 1918, when it appeared that the Romanovs would have trouble getting out of Ekaterinburg, McCully was still with the Atlantic Fleet off the coast of France and Riis was arriving in Russia. But there is an excellent chance that Koehler and possibly one or two American assistants were in Siberia and on their way to Ekaterinburg, if they hadn't already arrived. Commander Koehler's son, Hugo Gladstone Koehler of Riverside, Conn., told me: "All that my Father ever passed on to us about this period of his life in 1918 and 1919 was that he was busy in Russia rescuing a hell of a lot of people."

By October, 1918, when the Romanovs had been secretly removed from Ipatiev House in Ekaterinburg but seemed to be facing difficulties traveling to Odessa from the Japanese hideout, McCully and Riis were somewhere in the Russian hinterland, and so, in all likelihood, was Koehler. In October, McCully was named commander of U.S. Naval Forces in Northern Russia (the Murmansk-Archangel area). We know from other sources soon to be described that Riis had gone underground in the Bolshevik nation with the cover and papers of "Commissar Maxim Galinski." There can be little doubt that McCully organized the 1,800-mile trip from the Urals to Odessa with the help of his flagship *Olympia's* wireless resources — the trip okayed by President Wilson as an American responsibility — and that Riis and Koehler were his principal aides. The other Americans mentioned in the Chivers Papers were not necessarily from ONI.

McCully's opportunity to enjoy the facilities of the *Olympia* was short-lived. The old two-stack cruiser, which was famed as Admiral Dewey's flagship at Manila Bay, was sorely in need of repairs. She had been operating in North Russian waters since the previous May. On November 8 she sailed for Invergordon, Scotland, with forty-seven wounded American soldiers bound for transfer home and McCully, with the temporary rank of rear admiral, was left to make his headquarters wherever he could find a place to perch. One such perch was aboard the 975-ton converted yacht *Yankton*. He traveled all over the scene of his command which included harbors on the White Sea and adjoining gulfs. He went to Archangel, where the foreign diplomatic corps and American Ambassador Francis had set up shop; to Murmansk and to many towns and hamlets that led from Moscow along the railroad through Vologda. That's the Navy's story from records that haven't been locked in a safe. McCully stayed in North Russia from October, 1918 to July, 1919. That overlaps the entire period of the planning and execution of the Romanovs' long trek to Odessa from the Ekaterinburg area. Then he went to Paris as the Navy's representative on an Inter-Allied commission working on the naval clauses of the peace treaty.

In December, 1919 he was appointed a Special Agent of the Department of State and chief of a diplomatic mission to South Russia.

In those portions of their Navy records that were not kept secret, there are tip-offs to information withheld. For instance, the Saint Stanislas awards were made to McCully and Riis at a time (1919) after Czar Nicholas II had abdicated and was supposed to be dead. Long after the war, in 1927, when the then Rear Admiral McCully became Commandant of the Sixth Naval District at Charleston, S.C., and his life story was reviewed in the local press, an editor thought someone had made an error about an award personally bestowed by the Czar in 1919. He queried the Admiral about it. The Admiral assured him that no error had been made. He declined to elaborate. If the mystified journalist had pursued the matter he might have broken quite a story. McCully died June 13, 1951, six days short of his 84th birthday.

CHAPTER 14

NAVAL AGENT KOEHLER

Hugh William Koehler, though his upbringing was American, (St. Louis, Phillips Exeter, Harvard and Annapolis), always bore the image of a prince-in-exile who was making the best of it in rather drab surroundings. He seemed mostly too well-bred and well-groomed for democratic scenery. The incongruity was duly noted by his classmates right down the line. *Lucky Bag,* the Naval Academy's senior year book for 1909, comments on the page devoted to Koehler's years as a midshipman:

> "The glass of fashion and the mould of form,
>   the observed of all observers"
> > —Shakespeare
> "I am not in the roll of common men"
> > —Shakespeare

The prose profile goes on to remark: "To look at him one would think he was a poet! One of the select fussers — the leader of the '400.' He and his 'American Beauties' make quite a hit with the ladies . . . has made enemies, but they respect him . . . a capable, conceited man who can't be bluffed."

But he held out the hand of friendship to his classmates, according to the *Lucky Bag*, via a well-stocked larder of tasty chow: "Is never without a good supply of eatables in his room, with doors open to all comers. Came into the Navy just to show what a 'Havuurd' man could do."

By the time Hugo graduated from the Academy in 1909, two skills had combined to give him that excessive amount of self-confidence which in a young man may be construed as sheer arrogance — often as unbearable arrogance. Skill number one was his repertory of social graces to which many girls quickly succumbed. Second was his unusual facility in mathematics. Nothing can better smooth a midshipman's course through examinations in navigation, gunnery, steam engineering, explosives, and the like, than a mind that finds all equations mere child's play. Conversely, an ineptitude in mathematics has cost hundreds of aspirants over the years their chance for naval commissions. Hugo breezed through his academic courses. He had more reasons than were good for him to be a super-assured young neophyte when he entered the navy right after graduation. One of Hugo's first assignments was as an aide to Admiral William S. Sims, an unsparing critic of the navy's programs. Admiral Sims had served on the China Station with a tour as intelligence officer of the Asiatic Squadron. In all likelihood he had something to do with reassigning the bright, young, multilingual Hugo Koehler to gunboat duty in China after Koehler had completed his first ONI indoctrination in Washington.

Not much has been handed down by his friends and family about his experiences on the Yangtze patrol other than that he enjoyed it. He had ample time to visit Russia's maritime provinces via the Chinese Eastern and Manchurian Railways. He went to Peking and Tientsin. He cased the Chinese towns and cities along the river. He roamed around the famous Bund in Shanghai where the foreign cruisers were anchored. Apparently he seized every chance to practice his linguistic powers among the French, Germans and Russians he met on the social merry-go-round, which included the Cricket Club and the officers' clubs.

By 1917 Sims, a flag officer, had become Commander of U.S. Naval Forces in European waters with his headquarters in London. Koehler was an aide to one of Sims's aides — Captain Arthur J. Hepburn. McCully was in Russia. Riis was in North Sea waters from which he would go to Russia when told.

But where was Koehler in actual fact?

Months before we entered the war he disappears like a dolphin from all the surface records and doesn't leap back into sight until weeks after the Armistice when he reappears in Odessa. The signs are persuasive that he was under ONI control and operating in Europe from a date close to that in which McCully took up his post at the American Embassy in Russia in 1914. It was some time prior to the U.S. declaration of war in 1917 that Koehler made his first visit to wartime Germany in the guise and uniform of a German Naval officer. That is the story understood by both his son, Hugo Gladstone Koehler, and his stepson, Senator Claiborne Pell. They are quite certain that Lieutenant Koehler's second "impersonation trip" to Germany was while the United States was at war. They believe it blurred in some manner into Lieutenant Koehler's later extended mission inside Russia.

"All my father ever told me about his experiences in Russia," Hugo Koehler said, "was that he was very busy rescuing people. As far as I can recall he didn't mention the Romanovs. I was too young to take in much that he said about Europe. I know he mentioned being chased by the Reds a great deal of the time. I remember him saying that on one occasion, when the Reds were coming, they had to blow up the mouth of a cave in which a great many valuables were hidden. I think he said there were lots of candlesticks and things like that. Perhaps they were gold candlesticks. Perhaps there were jewels, too.

"You see, my father died when I was eleven. I was really never old enough to question him about his adventures as a maturer person might."

His mother, Hugo William Koehler's widow, was the former Matilda Bigelow, first the wife of Herbert Claiborne Pell, former Congressman and N.Y. Democratic State Chairman who was U.S. Minister to Portugal and Hungary. He was vice chairman of the campaign for Franklin D. Roosevelt when the latter sought his second term for President. Mr. Pell died on July 18, 1961. He was the father of incumbent Senator Claiborne Pell (D., R.I.) born in 1918. After her divorce from Herbert C. Pell, and her remarriage to Hugo William Koehler, then a Naval Commander, in 1927, Matilda Koehler presided over a menage which consisted of three males — her husband, the Commander; her first son, Claiborne Pell; and her second son, Hugo Gladstone Koehler, born Sept. 3, 1929.

"From the time I was nine years old," Senator Pell informed me, "I lived most of the time, for ten months of each year, in the same house with my stepfather, Commander Koehler. I loved the man. He was a very gifted, very unusual person. On many occasions I have met people who knew something about his exploits and from them, as well as from my Mother and from what I could note myself, I have been convinced that a fine book could be, and should be, written about him. Whoever wrote it, however, would have to dig into areas where the facts are not easy to come by."

One word alone in Commander Koehler's service record enhances the importance of Senator Pell's admonition to dig. The one word in the record is "Warsaw."

After Koehler (and Riis, too) aided Admiral McCully on his mission as Special Agent of the State Department in South Russia, following the Armistice, Koehler was appointed U.S. Naval Attaché at Warsaw. Why? The 1919 edition of Jane's Fighting Ships states that "At present the Polish Fleet is only a project. . . ."

The time and place of Koehler's assignment are intriguing. Warsaw was not only one of the reported sites where ex-Czar Nicholas II, incognito, was conspiring to help Marshal Pilsudski support the Whites against the Reds across Poland's border with Russia; it was also the place where British agents Boris Savinkoff, Paul Dukes and Sidney Reilly had been sent for the same reason.

Had Koehler, by then a Romanov acquaintance, been quietly shipped to Warsaw to keep in touch with this underground operation?

The suggestion is heightened by the fact that Archbishop Pacelli (later Pope Pius XII) was also in Warsaw at the time from his post in Germany. He conferred on numerous occasions with the relatively junior Koehler on a subject which the latter would not disclose to his family.

From all the visible signs, Koehler and Riis also went on ONI assignments both before and after their retirements. Koehler, for example, spent months at the scene of the Spanish Civil War in the 1930s. His family understood this to be an ONI task. He made similar trips to England and Northern Europe. With an apartment at 510 Park Avenue in New York and a large farm at Portsmouth, R.I., where he wasn't far from the Naval War College at Newport, Koehler lived in what even an admiral might regard as high style.

The country place was known as "Eastover." The manor house commanded a fine view of the Sakonnet River, a salt water estuary that leads north from Portsmouth towards Fall River. Inside the house Hugo and Matilda Koehler had a cook and other servants. Outside they employed additional help and maintained, among other things, a truck, tractor and four automobiles, two of them of expensive foreign make. "Eastover" was a visiting mecca for Koehler's friends from Newport, many at the Naval War College. It could be reached by road, sail or powerboat.

During Koehler's forays to Europe he socialized with the nobility as well as with personalities in the foreign naval and military hierarchies. On occasions he lunched with certain members of the British Royal Family when he was in London. It was not until his obituary was published in June, 1941, with the Navy on the verge of another war, that his friends learned of the extent of his connections in the Mediterranean and Eastern Europe. In this obituary which his widow, Matilda, helped to prepare, appeared this paragraph:

"He was later appointed naval attaché at Warsaw, Poland, and during this period was sent to the Balkans. He became acquainted with Josef Stalin and the late President Kemal Ataturk Pasha of Turkey, and was decorated by several governments for conspicuous services in a Turkish dispute. He was awarded the Navy Cross by the United States Government and was made a commander in both the French and Belgian Legions of Honor. From 1926 to 1927 he was attached to the staff of the Naval War College at Newport, retiring shortly afterward."

This is, to put it mildly, quite a round of contacts and attainments for an American naval officer of very modest rank.

Fittingly enough, it's the daughter of an admiral — with her own reputation as a dynamo — who probably knew Hugo Koehler better than anyone now alive: Mrs. Margaretta "Maggie" Potter of Jamestown, Rhode Island. She met Hugo in April, 1921 in Washington, when her father brought him home to dinner. "My friendship with Hugo Koehler covered twenty years," she said, "from the moment I met him shortly after his return from an assignment in South Russia, until his death in June, 1941. I think I knew him better and saw him more truly than did most of his other friends.

"He was a puzzle for two reasons: his brain was vastly superior to our brains, and he simply did not fit into the American scene. Physically he was not tall, but squarely built and very strong. When he walked, with rather short steps, he carried his head high, slightly thrown back, and he never watched his feet, as Americans invariably do. He was strikingly handsome, even in his last years, when he was not well, and his hair had turned white and his waist had thickened.

"He spoke English in his deeply pitched voice with a faint Germanic accent. He was one of the best raconteurs and conversationalists I have ever listened to, although this very excellence led him to the sin of pontificating, and when there was no one well-informed enough for him to sharpen his wits against, he could be really insufferable.

"His grandfather, who had been a gentleman at the court of Franz Josef before he emigrated from Vienna to St. Louis, seems to have overseen Hugo's education carefully. He took his grandson to Austria every summer and insisted that he attend Harvard for at least two years before going to the Naval Academy — 'the Naval Academy is only a training, not an education,' he said.

"The navy was the springboard of his activities, and in sending him to Germany and Russia during the World War I era, it gave him assignments whose challenges matched his abilities. He was reticent about his adventures during this period. He was ordered ostensibly as an observer, and I feel sure that his penetrating dark eyes missed very little, even without that corrective monocle. Perhaps some day his reports, still classified after fifty years, may be made public, and will prove how fearless and adroit an emissary the ONI and State Department had in Hugo Koehler."

During some of his assignments in Russia, Koehler masqueraded as an Armenian rug dealer, according to his friends and Mrs. Potter. Not long after she met him in 1921, Mrs. Potter said, he presented her with an ornate fan of ivory and lace whose predominant color is pale yellow. It is inlaid with mother-of-pearl. "It was a present from a Russian lady," he told her. He would never say who the lady was.

Maggie Potter cherished the fan and gave it to young Hugo Koehler's bride, Polly, as a wedding present. In light of what they have since learned, they are more curious than ever about the identity of the "Russian lady" who once owned it. The same applies to the original owner of a sumptous black sealskin overcoat which bears the trade mark of a St. Petersburg furrier and the date, 1912. It is now in possession of son Hugo. His father told him that he won it in a poker game somewhere in Russia, but always declined to name the man he won it from.

CHAPTER 15

AGENT SERGIUS M. RIIS

Sergius M. Riis, "the big bear with a soft voice," was born in Rome, N.Y., on September 30, 1883 of Danish parents. At the time of his birth his father was breeding silver foxes.

The urge to roam beset Sergius when he was still too young to shave. At the age of twelve he ran away to Boston and became a cook's assistant on a British windjammer bound for Australia. When it was discovered that the husky youth toiling in the galley had vastly exaggerated his age as well as his parents' consent to his travels, the captain graciously arranged with the U.S. consular authorities in Australia to have the runaway sent home and thence back to school.

For the rest of his life Sergius Riis, whom his friends called "The Skipper," seemed to be always blessed with the luck of finding some influential guardian angel who was willing to bail him out when another itch to see the world had run its course. For the first part of his life this luck derived from an uncle with powerful connections in New York and Washington. In later years his chief admirer and dispenser of favors was Admiral McCully. Riis probably had no more courage or daring than McCully and Koehler, but he certainly had more utterly deadpan, unmitigated gall. This was the quality for which the other two must have felt most indebted to him.

Young Riis's uncle was Jacob A. Riis, the Danish immigrant who became a crusading reporter on the *New York Sun,* campaigning for better housing and more parks for the city's poor. A friend and biographer of Teddy Roosevelt, Uncle Jake was the man for whom the Jacob A. Riis Neighborhood Settlement in New York City was named.

Around 1900 Sergius's father went to Russia in search of more furs and was granted honorary status as commercial attaché at the American embassy in St. Petersburg, probably at the behest of Theodore Roosevelt. It was there that young Sergius continued his studies and not only learned to speak Russian fluently, but acquired the slight foreign accent that never quite vanished from the English he spoke after he returned to the United States.

Sergius came back to his native land with the idea of going into the Navy or Merchant Marine. He had grown into a broad-shouldered, athletic figure of five-feet-eleven and 186 pounds. His bear-like appearance was enhanced by an ambling gait and massive head with wide cheekbones. His voice was exceptionally quiet until his interest was fired up. Then, like Koehler, but unlike McCully, his speech was rapid and voluble.

He attended the New York State Nautical College (now the State University of New York Maritime College at Fort Schuyler, the Bronx.) He acquired just enough skill with the sextant to wangle a job as assistant navigator, at the age of twenty-three, on the polar relief ship *Terra Nova.* This is the vessel that rescued the Fiala-Zeigler Polar Expedition of 1903–05 when it became lost in the ice off Franz Josef Land.

Back in the States once more he picked up rumbles of good news. The Navy was getting ready to expand under the leadership of Teddy Roosevelt, the apostle of the "strenuous life" to which young Riis himself aspired. Sergius seized a chance to enter the Marine Corps School of Application at Annapolis, in the shadow of the

Naval Academy. He served there for one year and emerged as a Marine second lieutenant in 1907. It was at a time when President Roosevelt and the Navy's General Board were drawing up plans for the world cruise of the "Great White Fleet," and the whole Naval Service was inhaling blasts of fresh air. Sometime in the following months Sergius Riis was chosen for duty in ONI and he traded in his Marine rank for that of Naval ensign. He received thorough training in Naval Intelligence practices and was promoted to Lieutenant, J.G.

After the United States entered World War I, Riis was sent to England with a mine squadron that helped the Royal Navy extend its mine barrage in the waters of the North Sea. Then, in the spring of 1918, he received the orders that turned the rest of the war into high adventure for him. He was transferred to the scene of his Russian school days. He was directed to report to the American Embassy in Petrograd (the St. Petersburg of his adolescence) as Assistant Naval Attaché. He had been there only a few weeks when the sky fell in on the whole foreign diplomatic corps and the Cheka, the Bolsheviks' secret police, began its wholesale slaughter of suspected foreign agents.

Riis burned his codes. He rushed to disguise himself and hide in the country.

For the story of his many months in Bolshevik Russia we are partially indebted to an account he wrote years later. It was published as a book in 1933 by Robert Speller & Sons of New York under the title *Yankee Komisar*. It begins in the late summer of 1918:

"I was in the office of the American Embassy in Petrograd when Hell broke loose outside."

Then his telephone rang. It was his friend, a Lieutenant Commander MacGloin, Assistant Naval Attaché at the British Embassy, an unexcitable man whose voice this time was "high and shrill." After identifying himself, MacGloin came to the point fast:

"And I'm telephoning to warn you," he said, "the Reds have just murdered Captain Cromie and slashed his guts out with bayonets. They're on their way now."

Riis needed no more information. It was the day after a young Social-Revolutionary girl, Dora Kaplan, had nearly assassinated Lenin by firing two pistol shots at him point blank, and Riis knew that the Cheka had launched a bloody riposte against all foreigners suspected of being involved in what the Bolsheviks called "the Allied Plot."

The principals of the U.S. Embassy were all in Vologda, 340 Miles north of Moscow. Riis made his decision to melt into the woodwork.

"I'd go further inland and trust to my wits to get me free," he wrote.

Thereafter the verve and pace of Riis's narrative are something like James Bond, Zane Grey and Richard Halliburton all rolled together.

He hurried to the Nicholaievsky Railroad Station in the hope of getting a train to Moscow. There he found thousands of others with the same idea. The station and its esplanades were jampacked. In addition to the live people were dozens of dead bodies stacked all over the place. The Red Guards had taken their toll there, too. Everyone was trying to get information about trains but there was no one to answer their questions.

Several trains, including short freights were standing on different spurs of track. Riis espied his friend Commander MacGloin in the crowd. MacGloin, it seems, had the same notion of leaving for Moscow.

They decide to offer money to the engineer of a locomotive attached to one boxcar on a siding. The engineer and his crew agree to rent their equipment to the two foreigners in an effort to see how far they can get from Petrograd.

They start off on the main line to Moscow. At first they are stopped by Red Guards about twenty versts from Petrograd (a verst is a Russian linear measure equal to about .6629 mile). They are allowed to proceed after displaying their passports. But fifteen versts further on they are halted by another cadre of Red Guards whose leader insists that they will be safer if he puts them under arrest and under the protective custody of two guards, Galinski and Morosov. This bearded pair had acquired the rudiments of English years before in New York's cloak and suit business. The Red Guard leader handed out papers to be delivered to the Commissar of the Cheka in Moscow.

Off they go again on their one-boxcar express to Moscow. As the train speeds through the night the guards fall asleep. Riis and MacGloin decide that the two sleepers planned to kill them at a fortuitous moment and take their money. They agree that they had better turn the tables before it is too late.

The two Westerners throttle the guards. A switch of uniforms, papers and passports is made on the floor of the careening boxcar. Riis and MacGloin implant their own uniforms and documents on the Russians' bodies. They put on the latters' clothing. They shave off the beards on the bodies and push them from the moving train, first taking care to douse the light on the rear of the boxcar so that no one at trainside could see what was up; or, rather, what was down.

From that moment, and for months afterwards, Lieutenant Sergius Martin Riis of the U.S. Navy operated all over the chaotic surface of Bolshevik Russia, according to his own chronicle, as Commissar Maxim Galinski. The latter, as it turned out, had been quite a wheel in the Bolshevik Party of old St. Petersburg. Riis was in constant dread of being exposed by someone in the Eastern Provinces who knew what Galinski looked like. For the remaining months of his stay in Russia, Riis's general course was through Moscow to Vologda to Kazan to Kiev to Odessa. He lost track of MacGloin and didn't rejoin him until they both had reached the environs of the Black Sea.

Riis would have his readers believe that his madcap sightseeing tour was simply to take intelligence soundings. In later chapters he draws vivid pictures of a plundering Bolshevik bandit named Kedrov living a de luxe existence in a private railroad car parked in Vologda; of Leon Trotsky in a special train loaded with liquor and cigarets for his officers near Kazan; of the Cossack General Semyon Budenny whom he went through the motions of helping to lure over to the Red's side.

(Budenny, later a Marshal of the Soviet Union, *did* shift his allegiance to the Reds after the collapse of General Deniken's anti-Bolshevik forces in the Ukraine. Riis offers a masterful study of Trotsky as a nimble psychologist who knew exactly how to rid the Red Army of all the old Czarist trimmings, trappings and customs from the epaulets to crowned eagles, and thus broaden its appeal to aristocrats and commoners alike.)

There is not a date in Riis's book from start to finish. One must supply one's own dates. (The attempted assassination of Lenin and the Reds' murder of Captain Cromie are, of course, well-documented.) Riis's gazette brings him no closer to Ekaterinburg than Kazan, a Tatar city about 350 miles away by rail. He makes no mention of the Romanovs anywhere, though he does state that he received a mission from the Cheka boss in Moscow to bring in some "important political prisoners" from the East whose lives must be zealously protected. No names are given. That's as teasingly close to anything like the Romanov rescue as Riis permits himself to go — and he puts the directive in the mouth, of all people, of the Moscow commissar of the Cheka. It is perfectly possible that this commissar *did* know at the time of Lenin's desire to extricate the Imperial Family from Siberia.

But there is a generous array of circumstantial evidence that Riis pointedly omitted all references to his real mission. In the first place, Navy Crosses are not often, if ever, awarded to someone who absents himself from his post through a mere whim to look around and see what was going on. As an assistant naval attaché, Riis's duty station — unless otherwise ordered — was with the American Embassy, first at Vologda, later at Archangel. He cites no command to go elsewhere. So in this respect his whole peregrination, and his stated reason for it, strain a reader's credibility.

Likewise his whole itinerary based on the sequence of events after Cromie's murder in the British Embassy has him making his swing way out to Kazan, on the banks of the Volga, and thence down to Kiev and Odessa, all at suitable places and times for him to help organize the Romanovs' trip from the Japanese hideout to Odessa, and to have shared in the journey. He, too, according to his book, arrived at Odessa in midwinter, when blocks of ice were floating in the harbor. He, too, by his own account, held a reunion in South Russia with some of his old British friends and an unidentified American "vice-consul." He, too, escaped from Odessa on a merchant ship even though there were by his own testimony two American destroyers not far offshore. His own version of the eastern terminus of his wayfaring was Kazan. That is only a day's trip on the railroad to Ekaterinburg (now Sverdlovsk). The distance is even less to Kungar where the Chivers Papers put the Romanovs at the end of December, 1918.

There are more touches which tend to move Riis closer to the Chivers Papers. One suggests that he may have written some of the messages himself. When the Romanovs left Kvalynsk, according to the Chivers message of Jan. 31, 1919, they were joined by eight American civilians "with Marine training." The reader will recall that Riis had received Marine training at Annapolis. If he was one of the eight who joined the party at Kvalynsk, the other seven were probably regular U.S. Marines in civilian clothes. Another clue is simply a phrase in the Chivers dispatch of Sept. 22, 1918. In it Nicholas is quoted as expressing fears that any American unit sent to help him would be infiltrated by elements of Russian refugees who would be only too glad to "bump them off." According to Riis's friends, this was one of his favorite terms. It is very doubtful that Nicholas himself used it.

A third is the language used in Riis's Navy Cross citation in 1920. Koehler won a Navy Cross for specific heroic action on a submarine assignment, but the citation for Riis was uncommonly vague. This award is the Navy's highest for valor, generally in combat, generally in the close physical presence of an enemy. Yet in Riis's case there is no mention of valor, combat or enemy. Here's the text:

THE SECRETARY OF THE NAVY
WASHINGTON

11 November 1920

SIR:—

The President of the United States takes pleasure in presenting the NAVY CROSS to

LIEUTENANT SERGIUS M. RIIS, USNRF
for services during the World War as set forth in the following:
CITATION:
"For distinguished service in the line of his profession attached to
various vessels of the U.S. Naval Forces in Northern Russia, acting
Naval Attaché to the American Embassy, at Archangel."

For the President

Josephus Daniels (signed)
Secretary of the Navy

Riis's friends assumed that his Navy Cross really was awarded
for bravery above and beyond the call of duty on a secret mission
that couldn't be defined. Undoubtedly they were right.

In World War II Sergius Riis was sent off on more missions of a
clandestine nature. In between assignments, and after the war, he
worked in the New York offices of the American Red Cross. Some
time in the late 1950s, when he had reached his seventies, he found
a home for himself on Staten Island which is in sniffing distance of
the ocean breezes. From there he came to the Red Cross offices by
ferry, enjoying the sights and sounds he loved — the inbound and
outbound vessels of the port, the hiss of tumbling water, the ships'
bells, the deep whistles. Late in February, 1963 he became seriously ill. It was from his death-bed that he came up with a tantalizing epilogue on the story of the Romanovs.

The date of his last illness came shortly after Mrs. Eugenia Smith
delivered the manuscript of her *Anastasia* autobiography to the
publishing firm of Robert Speller & Sons. Her manuscript recounted
how Anastasia had escaped the brutal "assassination" which ended
the lives of the other six members of the Imperial Family. The
Spellers were then considering whether or not to publish it. They
had been appraising the work for some time and it seemed convincing. It checked out with related facts familiar to the Spellers'
from the firm's more than thirty years of specialization in books by
Europeans, or about European affairs.

Then came word to them that Riis was ill. Jon Speller, Vice

President of the firm and son of the publisher, was a close friend of the old and ailing naval agent on Staten Island. Years before the two had worked together from first to last page of Riis's *Yankee Komisar*, and on other works at subsequent dates. Jon decided to phone Riis, on hearing of his illness, and try to cheer him up. Jon's Mother, Maxine Speller, was also fond of Riis. She chose to come in on the phone call from another extension.

They got Riis on his bedside telephone. His voice was faint; his words faltered, but he inquired about their health and asked what was going on at the firm. Jon told him about the *Anastasia* manuscript. He listened at some length. Finally he asked:

"You say she claims to have escaped, but that the others were all murdered?"

"That's right," said Jon.

"Then she's a fake . . . none of them were murdered," said Riis.

"You mean they all escaped?"

"Yes . . . they all escaped."

Jon and his Mother exchanged uncertain glances. Too bad for the poor old Skipper, they thought. He was really ill.

"How do you know they all escaped?" Jon asked.

The reply was delayed, but when it came it was the one vigorous assertion that Riis made in this exchange.

"I know . . . I know," he said.

His words were construed by both Jon and Maxine Speller as an index of how much his faculties had slipped towards senile nonsense. Both resolved to go out to Staten Island and visit him for old times sake. They didn't move fast enough. Several days later (March 12, 1963), he died. A few months after, Lt. Col. Michal Goleniewski, the Polish defector, arrived at the Speller offices with his account of the escape of the Romanovs from Ekaterinburg. It was a story which completely substantiated Riis's parting remarks.

"I will always kick myself for my reactions to what the Skipper told us that day," Jon Speller said. "I should have gone right out to Staten Island to see him. I had spent weeks of my life in his company and never once had the subject of the Romanovs' fate been broached. We had a close relationship. Considering the years of our friendship, the generations that had passed since the Romanovs were in Ipatiev House, the coming of Eugenia Smith, the short time that the Skipper knew he had left, I am sure he would have told me what he knew. I believe my failure to respond was one of the greatest mistakes of my life."

Sergius Riis left one son and only child, Earl Riis, who now lives in Florida. For all the years that he can remember, his father had an obsessive fear of being stalked and shot by Red agents in reprisal for something he did in Russia. After Leon Trotsky was murdered in Mexico on August 20, 1940, this trepidation increased, Earl told me. "Whenever I met a girl and introduced her to him, he was always very suspicious of her," said Earl.

Similarly, in social gatherings, especially in public places like restaurants and hotels, Sergius was relentless in inquiring into the backgrounds of persons who joined his group unexpectedly. Often it took him so long to verify them that it was embarrassing for all concerned. The new arrivals would be subject to unconcealed signs of coolness and even hostility.

"My father was a very secretive man," Earl observed. "He was particularly secretive about what he had done in Revolutionary Russia. He kept a lot of papers in his apartment, but before he died he made me destroy them. A few days after he died, in 1963, a rather mysterious thing happened. I was working in New York at the time and living with my mother in Brooklyn. One morning I walked out of the door and found in front of it, on the floor, a package wrapped in brown paper. It contained a long, typed biography of my father bound in red leather with gold markings. The biography was written in the third person, as if someone else was the author. That could be true, too. One by one I asked all of his friends whom I knew if they had dropped it off. All the answers were negative. To this day I have no idea how that leather-bound booklet got there."

It is not only from Earl Riis, but from this anonymous biography of his father, that the following facts have come to light:

Like Hugo William Koehler, Sergius Riis went to Poland in the 1920s. He arrived after Koehler left, but stayed much longer, and became a protégé of Marshal Jozef Pilsudki.

Like Koehler, Sergius Riis was invited often to Buckingham

Palace on his visits to England. He became "well-acquainted" with King George V. On one of his calls at the palace, one of the King's granddaughters — "a little girl nicknamed Lillibet" — came into the room "and gave the King a kiss." Before she left she kissed Riis, too, the biography relates. (Lillibet is now Queen Elizabeth II — born on April 21, 1926.)

Again, like Koehler, Riis met in Moscow some time between 1918 and 1920 — according to his biography — "the quiet, unassuming young secretary of the Central Committee, Joseph Stalin."

Duly noting that the sequestered Romanovs probably were in Poland in the 1920s and 1930s, and that Marshal Pilsudski and his Polish underground were focal points of anti-Communist intrigue, it is not impossible that Riis and Koehler — both persons whom Nicholas could trust — were used, in addition to their other missions as couriers, around an orbit that included among its way stations King George V and British Intelligence; the Polish coalition; Naval Intelligence and State Department Intelligence. It should not be forgotten that Admiral McCully served after World War I in South Russia as a special agent for the State Department, and chose Riis and Koehler as his assistants. Riis's later arrangements in Warsaw on the Polish-British-American network, taking the cover of an oil company representative, could have endured successfully until the death of Marshal Pilsudski on May 12, 1935.

The biography left with his son shows an almost continuous link with U.S. intelligence agencies and Allen Dulles, former CIA Director, from post-World War I days to the time of the Beria-Stalin plots in the 1950s. Many of the sequences in the biography follow the narrative in Riis's own book, *Yankee Komisar*, which contains the same story of Riis's seizure of the papers and identity of "Commissar Galinski." The only minor difference is the name of Riis's fellow adventurer from the British Embassy. In the book the British naval officer is "MacGloin." In the biography it's "McClaren." In the latter there is the same reference as in the book to being assigned to deliver "some important political prisoners" from Kazan to Moscow, an assignment which the biography states he carried out by proceeding "through Vologda." The biography is thirty-one pages long. It contains two excellent photographs of Riis, one of them in Navy full dress. It eventually delivers him to Odessa where he has to wait for a "new assignment."

Earl Riis came to New York and read the Chivers messages. He agreed with his father's friends that there were many phrases and expressions in them which smacked of Sergius M. Riis's manner of writing English.

"The style is very reminiscent of my father," said Earl. "He had a feeling for the flavor of words, and rather than use short ones, he favored the more formal or more lengthy ones. People would find him a bit more wordy than average." Earl was particularly struck (as suggestive of his father's authorship) by the more convoluted sentences in the dispatch of February 17, 1919: ". . . but to our despair yesterday to Church they did insist upon to attend" and ". . . all were moved to gratitude and some to tears, relief and respectful affection mixing."

Because of his father's innate taciturnity on the subject of his Naval Intelligence career, Earl says that he is not surprised he is learning more and more about that career, as the years go by, from others. The whole story is only beginning to take shape, as far as he is concerned. He would welcome any more information that might be offered. He would be especially pleased, he says, if the person who dropped off that biography at his doorstep would make himself (or herself) known.

There are too many gaps in the data now available about the three Naval agents to make a foolproof reconstruction of their roles. There is a lot of solid information about them, however — gaps in the gaps, so to speak — on which to base enlightened surmise.

All three were in the area. All three spoke several languages, including Russian. All three had been trained professionally by the Office of Naval Intelligence. All three were closely associated. At least two of the three — McCully and Riis — were recorded by others in a conference during a hurried visit by Riis to Vologda in the late spring or early summer of 1918. All three received subsequent assignments as special agents of the State Department. Thereafter two of them — Riis and Koehler — became frequent visitors at Buckingham Palace which was unusual for a pair of junior and rather obscure American Naval officers. Two of them were later assigned to Warsaw, which was the center of the Marshal Pilsudski–Winston Churchill anti-Communist underground to which the ex-Czar Nicholas was reportedly lending his influence — with the help of British Agents Sidney Reilly, Paul Dukes and Boris Savinkoff. It is not a wild assumption that, by this time, the personal contacts they had had with Nicholas had something to do with Riis and Koehler going to Warsaw as well as to Buckingham Palace. Not far away in Denmark, until her death in October, 1928, was Nicholas's mother, the Dowager Empress Marie, at Hvidore Palace. There is no proof that they visited her — and none that they didn't. (It is an interesting fact that Secretary of State Charles Evans Hughes's special representative, Roy C. Woods, came and went from Warsaw on his mission to deal with Tatiana five years before Marie died.)

Riis's friends, as well as his son, claim to recognize several of his language idiosyncrasies in the Chivers messages. Phrases they spotted were "naught was understood" and "bump them off" in the dispatch of September 22, 1918. (Mr. Bessell didn't put the latter phrase in quotes when he paraphrased this message, but he assured me that it was there. According to Jon Speller, the American gangster expression was one of Riis's favorites.) Also "attendant risks" in the dispatch of October 9, 1918; "attendant expulsions" in the dispatch of January 20, 1919, and "but to our despair yesterday to Church they did insist upon to attend" in the dispatch of February 17, 1919.

We know that Riis arrived in Russia in the Spring of 1918, long after the American Embassy had moved to Vologda (in February). We learned from his own book, *Yankee Komisar*, that he was in Petrograd when "all hell broke loose" (after Dora Kaplan had shot Lenin and Cheka gunmen had murdered the British Naval Attaché, Captain Cromie — August 30 and 31, respectively).

Since Riis was operating independently, and since the railroads were running in July, he very well could have been in Ekaterinburg in time to file the first of the Chivers messages on July 10, then returned to Petrograd; then returned to Ekaterinburg.

All of this, plus other evidence, leads to these hunches:

Riis and Koehler were "agents" assigned to the rescue party.

Admiral McCully was the supervising "agent" who coordinated the Americans' efforts with those of other nations.

In performing this function, McCully remained in this theater as Commander of U.S. Naval Forces in North Russian waters. He represented President Wilson in the rescue. He, in turn, assigned his own hand-picked sleuths, Riis and Koehler, to the execution of the plans. It is possible that McCully made at least one visit to the Romanovs in their Japanese hideout, for he would have had easy access to Ekaterinburg by rail from the north until the line was cut later in the summer.

Waiting in the Japanese compound from July to December, which was also a wait for the Allies to establish their beachhead at Odessa, there wasn't much for the message sender to do. As soon as the trip to Odessa started, however, there was need for more U.S. manpower — and it materialized.

Riis and Koehler were responsible for dealing with eleven other Americans who came into the Chivers picture at various stages. Three were the Americans who visited the Japanese compound intent on overhearing the private conversation of Nicholas and Alexandra. They are described in the message of September 22, 1918. Eight more, "American civilians with marine training," are logged as additions to the party after it left Kvalynsk, and clearly this group (probably U.S. Marines in mufti) must have been led to the junction point by someone. Perhaps it was Koehler, for thereupon the message sender gives a roster of the escorts as twenty-four guards, two servants, plus two U.S. Government agents. The last sound like Riis and Koehler. All this is recounted in the message of January 31, 1919.

It is likely that American Ambassador David R. Francis was kept in ignorance of the rescue, or only belatedly informed. In the first place, his entourage was suspect. The Ambassador's long friendship with an attractive matron, Matilda de Cram, nicknamed "Frau von Cram," was the source of Allied Intelligence reports that he was in the toils of a German spy. That gave diplomats of several nations an excuse to by-pass Mr. Francis on all matters of vital import. The State Department was fully aware of these rumors. So, probably, were President Wilson and Colonel House. Neither would have wanted to risk any leaks about Chivers. Secondly, Mr. Francis, a former governor of Missouri, was not regarded as one of the great minds of his day. British Agent Bruce Lockhart, after dining with Mr. Francis at Vologda, entered this note in his diary: "Old Francis doesn't know a Left-Social Revolutionary from a potato." All the more reason to keep Chivers under the tight control of a bright, disciplined professional long versed in Russian affairs, and a man whom President Wilson knew — Admiral Newton A. McCully.

Riis, joined somewhere by Koehler, made the trip with the Romanovs to Odessa. Like the other Americans, they were probably arrayed in civilian clothes. Koehler told some of his friends that he was dressed in Russia, in 1918 and 1919 for part of the time, as "an Armenian rug merchant." To an American lady friend who was about to be married (and who asked not to be identified), he presented some gems which he suggested that she have set in a ring. Pulling them out of his pocket almost casually, he said: "They're some stones I picked up in the Urals."

One doesn't have to strain to see how their personal links to the Romanovs may have shaped the Riis and Koehler careers for years afterwards. They were the two Admiral McCully specifically asked for as assistants when he was moved from North Russia to South Russia as not only Commander of U.S. Naval Forces, but as Special Agent of the State Department. They also took the Warsaw station in relays — first Koehler, as U.S. Naval Attaché in 1922; later Riis, in the cover of a civilian, through the late 1920s and well into the 1930s.

They were undoubtedly important American contributors to the anti-Communist Polish underground fashioned by Marshal Pilsudski and which flourished long after his death in 1935.

Though it failed to crush Bolshevism, it helped to inflict defeat after defeat on the Red Army at the approaches to Warsaw in 1920, under the tactical leadership of French General Maxime Weygand.

It was the Polish underground which pushed the nation close to kicking over the traces in 1956, the year of the Hungarian insurrection.

It was the Polish underground that provided the West — through Lt. Col. Michal Goleniewski — with information leading to the exposure of KGB men all over the world in the 1950s: Stig Wennerstroem, Gordon Lonsdale, George Blake, Dr. Israel Beer, William John Vassall, and many more.

It was from the Polish underground that Colonel Goleniewski, suddenly endangered by exposure himself, fled to West Berlin on Christmas Day, 1960, bringing updated news of Nicholas's survival and ultimate death in 1952.

It seems to have been the Polish underground that tipped off Sergius Riis to the oncoming Hitler-Stalin Pact in pre-World War II days, and to Beria's plan to step into Stalin's shoes in post-World War II days. They were tips that he passed on to Washington, as recorded in the biography left with his son, Earl.

And again, in a story only released on Nov. 10, 1974, it appears to have been the Polish underground which enabled the British to break the ciphers of high-level Nazi military signals in World War II. The coup became known as "Ultra." It resulted from the collaboration of a young Polish mechanic, expelled from eastern Germany in 1938, who was able to convince Britain's Secret Intelligence Service agents in Poland that he had been working on an improved German mechanical cipher machine — a system of electrically connected revolving drums around which were scattered the letters of the alphabet. A typewriter fed the letters of a message into the machine, where they were scrambled by the drums. An incoming coded message could be likewise unscrambled by the machine. It was known by the Germans as "Enigma." Churchill called "Ultra" his "most secret source," according to former SIS agent Fred W. Winterbotham, in his book, *The Ultra Secret*. Gen. Eisenhower termed it "of priceless value." The Polish mechanic was rushed to Paris in the late 1930s. There, mock-ups of the machine were made and later perfected by the British and Poles back in Warsaw.

Thus the Anglo-American investments in Marshal Pilsudski's aspirations, aborted as they were in the 1920s and early 1930s, may be reaping dividends for years to come. For the anti-Kremlin mood in Poland is far from moribund, according to the latest reports.

All told, then, it may have been the Romanovs who quite unwittingly — through Wilson, McCully, Riis, Koehler and other Americans — sparked our encouragement to the underground of a nation that has had to dream of independence for many, many years longer than it has ever been able to enjoy it.

These, then, are the men who most likely organized and carried out the Chivers operation as far as Odessa. There the British Navy took over the rescue. The story of these ships, their captains and crews are another chapter in this remarkable odyssey.

CHAPTER 16

A TALE OF TWO SHIPS

Happenstance has chosen a wide variety of sites to mark the moment when one era was being ushered out and another ushered in. Sometimes the locale has been a battlefield like Waterloo. Sometimes a cradle in the bullrushes. Or a brick house in Appomattox. Or a guillotine in Paris. Or a machine shop in Detroit.

Warships have had more than their fair share of the prestige of ceremonializing these great occasions. The Armistice with Turkey in World War I was signed aboard the British battleship *Agamemnon,* and, in World War II, the final capitulation of Japan was ritualized on another battleship, the U.S.S. *Missouri,* though the overriding presence there was an old dogface infantryman, General Douglas MacArthur.

Over the centuries, however, few naval vessels have served as sociological screening devices in the process of determining which personalities from a dying era should be rescued and carried into the next, and which should be left behind. Few have served, so to speak, as a Noah's Ark for a certain breed of humans. At the end of World War I such a role fell to several of the Royal Navy's largest craft and quite a few smaller ones. Little about their work was published at the time because the Admiralty was under fire from the British leftists for trying to save so many "Czarist aristocrats." Most notable of the vessels on the mission were H.M.S. *Agamemnon,* H.M.S. *Lord Nelson* and H.M.S. *Marlborough,* all battleships; the light cruisers *Calypso* and *Forward;* the destroyer *Acorn,* and the frigate *Grafton.* The little 4,120-ton *Calypso,* with her afterstack slimmer than the other, had been commissioned so late in the war that the Admiralty had to scrape the bottom of the manpower barrel to give her a crew. It turned out to be quite a crew. At least one — the captain's messenger, Hubert M. Limbrick, a former City Councilman of Thunder Bay, Ontario — is still alive as this is being written. He is quite certain that his vessel gave the Czar's daughter, Anastasia, a lift from the Black Sea to Venice under the chaperonage of an elder lady and Cossack guards.

Of the earliest British warships to pass east of the Bosphorus after Turkey lay down her arms, the cruiser *Calypso* probably had the most rough-and-tumble experience. She had her nose banged one way or another in most of the South Russian ports. She put into Sebastopol, Yalta and Odessa, and after helping in the rescue of the White Russians she returned to the Black Sea, as the *Marlborough* did, to pummel the Bolsheviks in the Crimea and to be pummeled, in turn, by their shore batteries. It was the *Calypso* that met boxcars filled with White Russian evacuees on the railroad pier in Odessa and carried them to safety. It was the *Calypso's* skipper, later Admiral Sir Bertram S. Thesiger, who personally manned and aimed one of the ship's 12-pounders that darkened a Red searchlight in Sebastopol, thereby enabling the cruiser to speed out of the harbor and escape the big guns trained on her. It was Thesiger for whom Hubert M. Limbrick served as messenger. He was blown from a gun-spotter's perch on the *Calypso's* foremast during a later firing duel with Red coastal batteries. He was wounded and hospitalized. He still suffers from the effects.

Limbrick joined the Royal Navy in September, 1917, at the age of fifteen. After leaving the training barracks at Shortley, he was assigned to the *Calypso* as the captain's messenger. The *Calypso* was almost as new to the Navy as Limbrick. A member of the *Cale-*

don class, with a rakish tilt to her masts and two funnels, she hadn't been finished in the Hawthorn Leslie yards until June, 1917. The three cruisers of her class became known as "Tyrwhitt's Dreadnaughts" by dint of the fact that they spent their first days of war service as units of the Harwich Force under Vice Admiral Sir Reginald Tyrwhitt. They could do thirty knots, and mounted five six-inch guns and eight torpedo tubes.

Limbrick, now seventy-two, is a retired civil servant living in Thunder Bay, Ontario. For many years he was a member of the City Council. Slim, of medium height, with merry eyes and white hair, he has endured for most of his life the pain and infirmities resulting from those moments fifty-four years ago when he was blown from the *Calypso's* foremast by a Red shell. He recently underwent major surgery.

What makes Limbrick a potential witness in the story of the liberation of the Romanovs is a series of incidents that started in Yalta in 1919. In the last days of 1918 the crew of the cruiser were given Christmas leave in England. Early in 1919 the ship was ordered to Malta. It made a trip to Fiume, up the Adriatic, to help the Italians recapture that city from the Austrians. Then, orders came to go to Sebastopol to meet a relief train loaded with women and children trying to escape the Bolsheviks. The Red infantry had taken salients around Sebastopol by the time the cruiser got there. News arrived that the relief train had been rerouted to Yalta. It was at Sebastopol that the searchlight had to be shattered by gunfire to insure the *Calypso's* nocturnal escape.

At Yalta, for the moment, everything was peaceful. The cruiser anchored in the beautiful harbor to await developments. Limbrick takes it from here in his own words:

"One day (at Yalta) while in my place outside the Captain's cabin, I noticed a very beautiful young lady about my own age in company with an older lady and two Russian officers who were rowing a boat around our ship. During the next two days they returned several times.

"I felt that they must be people of some importance, and reported them to the Captain. He seemed very interested and said that he would hail them to come aboard the next time I spotted them.

"In due course they reappeared and were invited aboard. The older lady seemed to be in very earnest conversation with Captain Thesiger, and when she introduced the young lady with her to the Captain, I could not help but notice the surprised look that came on his face. The visitors talked with Captain Thesiger for some time, and then he beckoned me to go to him. After I saluted each one personally, the Captain said: 'This young lady is a Princess Royal of the Russian Royal Family. I want you to escort her and her two officers on a visit over our ship.'

"Naturally I was delighted, and proceeded to lead the party. I presumed the Russians had no ships as new as ours because they seemed to be thrilled with everything they saw. They were especially excited about our beautiful engines, and why not? They were capable of thrusting our 4,120-ton cruiser through the water at thirty knots.

"The young lady was very gracious and spoke fairly good English, but with a heavy Russian accent. At my age, most of my education having been towards the nautical life, I did not know that the word 'Royal' was only attached to the title of members of a royal family. However, after I was discharged from the Royal Navy, and a civilian again, I realized that because the young lady I had escorted was addressed as the 'Princess Royal' she must have been a member of the Russian Royal Family who were all supposed to have been assassinated by the Reds!"

The *Calypso* stayed in Yalta for two weeks. Limbrick saw no more of the mysterious ladies there. A message came which reported that the Reds were now advancing on Yalta and that the relief train had been rerouted again — this time to Odessa. The cruiser was ordered to get there as quickly as possible. As the configuration of Yalta's cliffs faded away over the *Calypso's* white wake, Limbrick was positive that the "Princess Royal" and her elder escort would never enter his life again.

He was wrong.

It was the middle of the night when the cruiser arrived in the harbor of Odessa.

"There on the dock," said Limbrick, "stood an old steam engine with a number of boxcars behind it. No sooner had we tied up when the boxcar doors opened. Women started to climb out and run towards the shop. There must have been two hundred or more. Their once beautiful clothes were ragged, their faces dirty and most of them were almost starving. A lot of them broke down after they were safely on board. We fed them with something I'll warrant they had never eaten before — corned beef and bean stew. But to them I'll bet it tasted better than caviar!

"After most of them were aboard, I noticed our Captain step ashore in order to escort a wonderful-looking elderly lady and younger companion. These two were taken by him to his cabin, but because we all had our hands full getting the other ladies bedded down, and then going back to sea, I did not get a close look at the ladies who spent the night in the Captain's quarters.

"The next morning the Captain, who had slept in an auxiliary cabin, told me where his quarters would be for a few days because, as his messenger, I had to be within easy call. He also told me that the elder lady in his cabin was none other than the Grand Duchess Feodorovna, and the younger one accompanying her the Princess Royal, whom I had escorted on the visit to our ship."

Applying the British term "Princess Royal" to the Russian Court, where it was not used, but as Captain Thesiger probably understood it, it would have meant the senior of the Czar's four daughters, the Grand Duchess Olga. In 1919 she would have been twenty-four. But only the Grand Duchess Marie, born in 1899, and the Grand Duchess Anastasia, born in 1901, could reasonably have fitted Limbrick's description of being about his own age (seventeen) at the time.

Three persons in the orbit of the Imperial Family had the name "Feodorovna" associated with them. They were Nicholas II's mother, the Dowager Empress Marie Feodorovna, whose trip to England on the *Marlborough* and *Lord Nelson* we have already traced, and the two German-born sisters, the Empress Alexandra, Nicholas's wife, and Elizabeth, the Grand Duchess Serge, both of whom reportedly had been slain by the Reds before the *Calypso* ever reached the Black Sea. Both had adopted "Feodorovna" to follow their first names so that the Czarina called herself "Alexandra Feodorovna," and her sister "Elizabeth Feodorovna." The latter was known by the Czar's children as "Aunt Ella." But neither Marie nor Alexandra would have called themselves "Grand Duchess Feodorovna." They were not grand duchesses. They were in their own opinions, in the framework of 1919, respectively Ex-Empress or Dowager Empress, and Empress. That leaves Elizabeth as the likeliest possibility for the elder of the two women on the *Calypso*. She and her sister, Alexandra, were members of the German Hesse family. She had been widowed before the Revolution. She had become a nun in the Russian Orthodox Church. Her disfigured body reportedly had been found, after the Red uprisings, in a grave near Perm. Conceivably this "death" could have been as much of a subterfuge as the murder of the Imperial Family.

Limbrick went on to note that "All of the ladies other than the Grand Duchess and the Princess Royal disembarked from our ship at a port in Romania. We took the other two ladies to Venice, Italy, and our mission was accomplished."

If Limbrick is not in error on his dates and ports, it is noteworthy that these two women, whoever they were, were regarded by the Admiralty as important enough to occupy the time, fuel and manpower of a cruiser long enough to steam out of the Black Sea, through the Sea of Marmora, down the Aegean, into the Mediterranean, and then up the Ionian Sea and the full length of the Adriatic, in order to put them ashore in Venice. He said they stayed in the Captain's cabin for the whole trip. Since the *Calypso* had to return to the Black Sea, it entailed a round trip of about 4,400 miles. That's quite a little detour for one pretty girl and her attractive older companion! Especially when a nearby port in Romania (possibly Constanza, though Limbrick doesn't remember) was good enough for all the other women on board.

"Since that day," said Limbrick, "there has been worldwide controversy as to whether or not Anastasia was or was not assassinated with the other members of the Russian Royal Family. For my part I sincerely believe that she was *not!*"

One of the proudest moments of Limbrick's wartime service came only a few hours after leaving Odessa. In full daylight, with the *Calypso* steaming on the Black Sea, the ship was overtaken by a smaller one.

"A destroyer loaded with male civilians hove up close to us," said Limbrick. The destroyer was not British, and he doesn't remember her nationality, he said, but he *does* remember "that there was a lot of shouting back and forth between the two ships. When the male civilians, mostly Russians, I guess, found out that their womenfolk were aboard, they wanted to join them on the *Calypso*. They yelled for permission.

"I was standing near Captain Thesiger on the bridge. When he heard their request, he pointed to me and shouted back: 'See that young man. He's only seventeen but he's fighting for his country and he's fighting for Russia. You go back to *your* country and do the same.'"

Limbrick is sure that this was the kind of presence of mind, to say nothing of quick eloquence, for which Thesiger was soon to be promoted to flag rank.

If Limbrick is right about Anastasia being on the *Calypso,* there is no basic conflict here with the information in the Chivers messages and the Lord Hardinge letter. It will be recalled that although the Chivers dispatches bring all seven Romanovs to Odessa in the middle of February, the Lord Hardinge letter fails to mention Anastasia, as well as Alexandra and Alexei.

Anastasia could very well have left the others at Odessa in February to visit her grandmother, the Dowager Empress Marie, at Yalta (Marie didn't leave there until more than two months later.) Then, when the advancing Reds raised a new problem, she could have hurried back to Odessa to hitch a ride from the Royal Navy.

Limbrick was visited recently in Ontario by a five-man team from the British Broadcasting Corporation in London. They were in the process of preparing a documentary, "The File on The Czar." Producer Tony Summers and Reporter-Narrator Tom Mangold took along a number of photographs of the real Anastasia snapped before July, 1918. Most of them were group poses.

"I picked her out every time," said Limbrick. "I made a score of eleven out of eleven. I am now sure it was she."

He has not yet studied enough photographs of the Grand Duchess Serge, he said, to determine whether or not she was the older companion. "But I remember something else very clearly: Cossack officers guarded the Captain's cabin as long as those ladies were in it. One had a black bag strapped or chained to his arm. My station was at the Captain's quarters, too, and I tried many times to get this officer to tell me what was in the bag. I couldn't make him understand my question." The Cossacks left the ship at Venice, he said, with the ladies.

This trip to Venice in the April-May period, 1919, doesn't square with the Admiralty's public records. They put the *Calypso* in Venice in the summer of 1919 (July 23-26) after stops at Pola and Fiume. Limbrick said he remembers the second trip to Venice, too, but is adamant that the cruiser made the first trip there without stopping anywhere after leaving the Black Sea. "You don't forget something like that," he said.

If Limbrick is right, it won't be the first time in this investigator's experience that official documents pertaining to the Romanovs have been expunged, withheld or altered.

The ship of ships in the whole armada, the one that in all probability removed the other members of the Imperial Family from Odessa and delivered them safely to foreign soil, reflected all the cunning touches that marked the Chivers operation up to the moment it reached the Black Sea.

She was what you would least except. She was not a battleship or a cruiser or a converted yacht with staterooms fit for a king. She had no luxurious furnishings inside or out. She was the kind of craft that attracts the least attention — that dirty-faced urchin of the seven seas, a merchant coal-carrier. She was not even a fleet collier like the 9,930-ton H.M.S. *Mercedes*, which had plenty of room in her officers quarters for gracious dining and salons out of earshot of rattling dishes. On the nautical social scale she was next to the very bottom. In that respect she embodied a paradox that should engage the attention of chroniclers of the great exodus for years to come. The highest-ranking figures in the old Czarist regime were carried away in the humblest kind of a hull. The needs for secrecy and camouflage were undoubtedly the reasons. But the dirty old coal-carrier with a Southampton registry had one endowment that linked her directly to the cockiest capital ships of the Grand Fleet: She had a Royal Navy crew, and it was the attention that might be attracted by this crew that most worried the British Secret Service, from all the sources and documents we have consulted.

In order to give the Admiralty the tightest possible control and security, SIS had deemed it necessary that before she put into Odessa with a load of coal, her regular skipper and civilian crew be replaced by R.N. personnel. The explanation to be given the French authorities in the port was that unsettled conditions there made it advisable that she be manned by seamen trained in the use of weapons.

The problem was, would that story go over?

It did.

According to the SIS plan, the ship's crew were to be given no inkling of the identity of the refugees who sailed out of Odessa with them. The seven Romanovs were heavily disguised and dressed to suit the lowly accommodations they occupied. They were represented to be Russians from several different families.

The Bulgarian Version of this stage of the rescue makes the following points:

Just before the Romanovs were taken aboard, and after the cargo of coal had been unloaded, the captain of the ship summoned his crew. He told his men he had discovered that they had a chance to render a merciful service to a few Russian refugees. He had decided to give them a lift to a nearby port outside of Russia. The stopover was more or less on their way and would only delay them a few hours on the return voyage. The whole matter was handled as a last-minute, eleventh-hour, spur-of-the-moment decision that followed naturally after the ship's apparent main mission had been carried out, namely, that her coal cargo had been put ashore.

There was no fanfare of any sort when the Romanovs were embarked late in the evening from the wharf at Odessa in a ship's tender, as the Chivers Papers described. There were no ceremonies to mark anything special about their arrival in Burgas.

By precautions like these, the planners of the voyage dealt with two contingencies: 1) They tried to arrange for nothing to happen during the ship's appearance in two different ports that would make a casual observer look twice and grow suspicious, and 2) They tried to arrange for nothing to take place on the trip, either ashore or on shipboard, to make any of the crewmen later believe that there had been much more to it all than they'd been told. This precluded any prior refurbishings of the cabin space allotted to the Romanovs. That would have been a giveaway. It would have rendered the captain's story of a spur-of-the-moment's decision utterly incredible. From all available data, it now seems that the quarters made available to the royal escapees came from having the deck and engineering officers double up with each other, thus freeing two or three staterooms for Nicholas and his family.

In 1971, an employe of the Board of Trade in London stumbled onto the story of the coal-carrier's short but historic mission. He was researching the vessels requisitioned through the board for emergency service by the Admiralty in 1918 and 1919. There were scores of them, large and small. Almost invariably, when they were requisitioned, their civilian captains and crews went along with them.

After working on his assignment for a few days, the Board of Trade worker found something interesting. It was a sheaf of records on a vessel which had been requisitioned, with the stipulation that its crew be removed and retained ashore at full pay for a short period of time. Thereafter the captain, officers and crew would be returned to their ship. Other papers in the set indicated that a Royal Navy crew had been emplaced on board.

The documents didn't give the name of the ship, only a number. Other despatches in the same dossier yielded the impression that the vessel had been involved in a secret service mission, the nature of which was pointedly not stated. The best he could gather from the papers was that she was fitted out for coal carrying; was of Southampton registry, and was small enough to be somewhere between 2,000 and 5,000 tons.

It so happened that a week or two after this researcher's discovery, the London newspapers broke out in a spate of letters to the editors about the Romanov Case. Odessa was mentioned in one or two of them as the probable port of embarkation. Quite enthused about his own find, the Board of Trade man made contact with one of our group in London, and was encouraged to go back and try to find out more about the ship in question with the possible aid of the Admiralty. That may have been the wrong move, however, and the reason for a quick cut off.

Our contact with the men in the Board of Trade was soon severed. An official of the agency offered no explanation other than venturing that "perhaps a mistake has been made."

That's a very equivocal observation. It can apply to almost anything. The researcher apparently had been ordered to butt out of the affair.

Something less than total credence was attached to the account of the Board of Trade researcher until the Bulgarian Version reached us a few months ago. It conformed in many respects with his: a coal-carrier, Royal Navy crew, the captain's story, the stop at Odessa, the night-time boarding, etc.

Then we took it more seriously. Here was the same account from two different sources. A hunt is now being made for the name of the ship and living survivors from the crew. If there are any, and they read about the identities of the Russians they lifted from Odessa, they should make themselves known. A great many persons would like to talk to them.

The ships already mentioned were by no means alone on the mission of saving fugitives from the Reds. French and Greek warships were with the British when they poked through minefields in the Turkish Straits in October, 1918. The Turkish surrender had preceded the German. Mines in all directions made the Allied fleet proceed with the utmost caution. Engine room telegraphs changed constantly from "slow ahead" to "stop engines" and the progress was so tedious that spectators watching around the Golden Horn thought the busy minesweepers were the only craft that were going anywhere. The naval vessels were followed by a ragtag squadron of merchantmen. Some of these had been mobilized by the Admiralty and given naval designations.

The men of this expedition were destined to witness scenes of extreme ferment. In the continuing White-Red battles, much of Southern Russia was still up for grabs. Bolshevik columns had already pushed into many strategic areas along the Black Sea's northern coast. The situation was changing daily. The Allies' Big

Four were debating among themselves whether to mount a full-scale assault on the Bolsheviks (though President Wilson was the least disposed to think along these lines). Factions of the Whites were feuding with each other. Patrols of Cossacks were taking orders only from leaders of their own choice. To confuse the shore-side operations still further, after the Kaiser fled to Holland and Germany surrendered, numerous detachments of the German Army milled around South Russia — as mentioned previously — looking for the proper authorities to accept their capitulation, and with it the responsibility for feeding them.

CHAPTER 17

UNDERGROUND

The Romanovs' "assassination" in 1918 ultimately produced over the years a whole new literature of fairy tales which could have done credit to Jonathan Swift, the brothers Grimm or Lewis Carroll. Indeed, putting together all the Romanov stories that have cropped out in the last fifty years would make multiple extensions of Hans Christian Andersen's first great volume, "The Ghost at Palnatoke's Grave."

What rugged and determined ghosts they were!

That of Anastasia alone was bewitching enough for a play, a movie, several books and any number of magazine articles and newspaper features. Two women who have nothing but sneers for each other's pretensions have fought hard for recognition as the Czar's youngest daughter, and the resulting literary fallout has been stupendous. They are Mrs. Anna Anderson Manahan and Mrs. Eugenia Smith. Mrs. Manahan lives in Charlottesville, Virginia, and Mrs. Smith in New York City. Clearly one must be a fraud. And even if one is genuine, both have been guilty of stretching the truth beyond the breaking point about those last days at

Ekaterinburg. Lately, for some reason, both ladies have remained silent.

The Anastasia tales are the ones best known to the general public, but on the less boisterous, more whispered, network of titled personages, there have been numerous accounts of the comings and goings incognito of Nicholas, his son, four daughters, his brother (the supposedly slain Grand Duke Michael) and his sister-in-law (the also supposedly slain former Grand Duchess Serge, better-known by Nicholas's children as "Aunt Ella").

In this milieu, the secret travelogues of the deceased have had Nicholas and one of his daughters visiting the ailing Woodrow Wilson in Washington, shortly before his death. On another gazette of the insiders, the former Grand Duchess Marie, Nicholas's daughter, was spotted on a long stay in a hotel in Venice in the 1920s. Both Nicholas and Alexandra were encountered in 1923 walking together near the basilique de Notre Dame de la Garde in Marseilles, from a letter written by William Rutledge McGarry. According to the book by Kenneth Roberts called *I Wanted to Write*, Marie's sister, Tatiana, was secreted in a Polish village from which she made sorties in the process of negotiating the sale of family-owned paintings and art objects which had been hidden from the Bolsheviks somewhere in Poland. Other sources later had Marie domiciled, first in a Polish village, later in Warsaw. Their sister Olga, as late as the early months of World War II, was said to be serving as a medical sister in a church-run hospital somewhere near the Russo-German front. Later Olga and Tatiana were reputedly married to Germans and residing in or near Frankfurt.

On this same network of Romanov insiders, the former Grand Duke Michael was placed in a home near his son, George, both under assumed names somewhere in Europe, and both were visited occasionally by Michael's wife and George's mother, the Countess Brassova (she had been taken to England on the British Battleship *Agamemnon*). Many persons in London were sure that the aging and mysterious "Sister Martha," who for years was treated as a privileged personage in the household of the Grand Duchess Xenia, Nicholas's sister, was none other than the Grand Duchess Serge

("Aunt Ella"). Both she and Michael had been reported murdered by the Bolsheviks in 1918 near Perm.

As for the Czarevich, a number of self-asserted "Alexeis" cropped out from time to time in Europe and America. Perhaps the one taken most seriously by Romanov buffs was Eugene Nicolaievitch Ivanoff. A Polish reporter stumbled on him in 1927 and he was written up in both the Polish and French press as a possible Alexei, son of the Czar, living undercover in Pomerelia, Poland, under the care of a priest and a small panel of tutors. He was described as being of the same age as Alexei, bearing a close resemblance to him and also suffering from hemophilia.

Now along comes the Bulgarian Version to tell us that for a while at least some of the Romanovs, after they left Bulgaria, found a refuge near Bruges under the protection of Queen Elizabeth of the Belgians.

All this amounts to more clues than any one mystery really needs. How does one go about separating the good ones from the bad ones? A helpful hint in this connection comes from two different directions. One is the Lord Hardinge letter, and the other the account of Colonel Goleniewski. Both indicate that the party of seven Romanovs was split up.

This suggests that one or more members of the family may have gone to places never reached by the others. A great many locales far-removed from the others' itineraries may have been visited for a while by a Romanov masquerading as a poor refugee under a prosaic name, a stratagem rendered relatively simple by the fact that Europe, the Mediterranean and North African cities were flooded at the time by uprooted persons of all description. In short, any number of places could have received clandestine visits from a Romanov from 1918 on. Probably there soon will be some expert backtracking by the European press to fill in the gap between the present and that moment more than half a century ago when "a British ship" mentioned in the Chivers Papers carried off the seven fugitives from Odessa.

I may be wrong, but pending the uncovering of more facts, I am inclined to believe that Poland will prove to be the nation in which Nicholas, Alexandra and Marie spent most of their time after the

rescue. One of the least persuasive of these reasons is Kenneth
Roberts' story about Tatiana. A few paragraphs from it in Roberts'
own words are worthy of close study because they record the exact
flavor of the exasperating ambiguity and golden sunset fadeout
that in later years rewarded so many others who tried to pin down
the truth about some member of the Romanov family.

The paragraphs were written about Roberts' visit to Warsaw in
1923, although his book was not published until 1949. The "he" in
the first paragraph is Roy C. Woods, a former assistant states attorney, of Chicago, whom Roberts describes as "an elegantly
dressed Charles Dana Gibson-ish American" who carried a pearl-
handled revolver in his hip pocket."

Around midnight he weakened and admitted that he was engaged
in a venture which must for now remain a profound secret, but which
would, one of these days, intrigue not to say startle, the world.

Around two o'clock in the morning he broke down completely. He
was in Poland, he said, because after newspapers of the United States
had commented admiringly on his prowess as Assistant States Attorney, he had received a call from a New Yorker who represented the
Russian Royal Family. Before the Royal Family had met its end in the
Ekaterinburg well, the Tsar had exported from Russia a nest egg of
crown jewels and immensely valuable paintings, all of which were
now in a warehouse, crated and ready for shipment. Furthermore, the
representative said, the Tsar's daughter, Tatiana, had been helped to
escape Ekaterinburg by a sympathetic Bolshevik officer and, in peasant garb, made her way over the Urals, across Russia and into Poland,
where she was now living as a peasant with a peasant family. The
Russian representative, Woods said, had commissioned him to visit
Poland and arrange transportation to America for the jewels, the
paintings, the girl, the Bolshevik officer who had helped her escape,
and three Russian women who had accompanied her from Ekaterinburg.

It was, of course, true that American Intelligence Officers in Siberia (where Roberts had been) had repeatedly reported the rumor
that one of the Tsar's daughters had escaped, as Garland and I had
set forth in 'The Brotherhood of Man;' but Woods' story struck me as

fantastic. Why, I wanted to know, should a New Yorker bother to go all the way to Chicago and seek out Woods, when a thousand better qualified New Yorkers could have been sent on such a mission? Woods modestly said it was because of his reputation as an astute prosecutor.

Had he seen the girl? I asked. Certainly he had seen her. He saw her every week. He took a plane from Warsaw, landed near the village in which she lived, and went secretly by night to visit her. How, I wanted to know, could he be sure she was what she claimed to be? With that, Woods really took down his hair. In his wallet he had a picture of the Grand Duchess Tatiana, clipped from a magazine. There couldn't be any mistake about it, he insisted. The girl he visited every week was unquestionably the girl in the picture. He had gifts that she had given him, among them a gold cigarette case decorated with the double-headed eagle of Russia in white enamel surrounding a diamond the size of a bean. He had, he insisted, seen the packing cases containing the portraits and the jewels; some had been opened for him; he had handled the jewels, seen paintings, some by great masters, Van Dyck, Rembrandt, Holbein, Titian. If ever he could overcome the girl's fear of Bolshevik reprisal, he proposed to charter a steamer, load all the packing cases aboard it, and take Tatiana and her friends to America. Did she speak English? Certainly she spoke English. All the Tsar's daughters had had English governesses.

On the assumption that it isn't safe to overlook anything, I made a deal with him to be given exclusive rights to publish Tatiana's story serially in the Saturday Evening Post. I was to be taken along on a chartered steamer when Woods took her to America, and have the opportunity of interviewing Tatiana several hours each day.

In about a month, Woods thought, he would sufficiently overcome Tatiana's fear of assassination by Bolshevik agents, and persuade her to board a ship; meanwhile he would keep in constant touch with me.

Woods *did* keep in constant touch with Roberts until weeks later when, Woods reported, it had become apparent that he would never be able to persuade Tatiana to expose herself "to the vengeance of the Bolsheviks."

Famed author Kenneth Roberts is long since dead and for several years — as mentioned in Chapter V — we assumed that the colorful existence of Roy Woods had succumbed to the weight of years sometime back in the 1960s. That's what we were told in Illinois and Minnesota towns where he lived at various times after his retirement. When, to our astonishment, he was located in Scottsdale, Arizona, in 1974, by Mr. Samborski, our hopes picked up that we could get the full story of his mission to Poland in 1923. We were wrong again. Four tries — by myself, Tony Summers, Samborski and the latter's lawyer friend, Louis N. Blumenthal, another famed former Cook County prosecutor who has retired to Scottsdale — were unable to budge Mr. Woods much beyond this repeated rejoinder:

"I am 95 years old. I am on borrowed time. I could go to my grave in an hour or tomorrow. I have kept this to myself all this time and I am not likely to start talking at this late date."

A somewhat shrunken shadow of a once spectacular figure, he added that he had had five cataract operations in recent years and had been hospitalized three times after heart attacks. He said:

"I am totally deaf in one ear and have to wear a hearing aid on the other. My sight and hearing are very limited. I am not allowed to view violence in sports or TV shows. I have used many bottles of nitroglycerine."

But one day, on one of Mr. Blumenthal's visits when Woods seemed to be spryer than usual, he yielded a little more information. "If I was in a position to do so," he said, "I could assure that any book on this subject would be a bestseller."

Mr. Blumenthal further reported on this interview as follows:

"He said he saw Roberts only once in his life and then only for about thirty minutes; that one man, a former bodyguard of the Czar, was the only person present when he was talking to Roberts, and that this solitary personage was the so-called 'bevy of girls' mentioned by Roberts. He also showed me a photograph of a huge gold-plated star with a large diamond in the center inscribed 'Assistant State's Attorney, Cook County, Illinois' which, he said, facilitated his numerous trips across national borders and which was erroneously described as the Czar's gold cigarette case.

"He did say that any statement he might make would require corroboration by others and although few, if any, of the others were still living, it would still expose that which they had kept secret in their lifetimes. As he talked he would lose his breath, and even seem to lose consciousness momentarily, and when he regained his senses he would remark: 'You can see for yourself how distressed I get to even think about this thing.'"

That Mr. Woods was something of a mystery man, and a wealthy one, too, was established by Mr. Samborski's investigations. Woods didn't gain admission to the bar until he was 43 years old. In Rockford, Minnesota, where Woods spent many past summers before his doctor forbade further travel, he owns several buildings on the main street including one that houses the post office. The postal employees have been enjoined against disclosing his street address in Rockford and Scottsdale and his name doesn't show in the Rockford telephone book.

As mentioned previously, there's a chance that Cyrus McCormick, the Chicago-based head of International Harvester, is the man who sent Woods to Poland on what Woods told Blumenthal was "a confidential mission for Secretary of State Charles Evans Hughes."

Mr. Woods' wife, who is much younger than he, assured Blumenthal that her husband never talked to her about the Polish episodes in his life, and ventured that he never would.

All its vagaries notwithstanding, then, the Woods-Roberts saga seems to point another arrow at Poland as the place where the Romanovs spent the greatest number of years in exile. Other arrows are War Minister Winston Churchill's dispatch to Poland in the post-World War I years of the top British agents; Hugo Koehler's assignment as U.S. Naval Attaché in Warsaw; Archbishop Pacelli's conferences with him there; Goleniewski's reports of Nicholas's burial there in 1952; Goleniewski's defection from Poland in 1960, and the continued presence there of Maria, "The Woman in Warsaw," who claims to be Goleniewski's mother. She may be the former Grand Duchess Marie, daughter of the Czar.

There is another reason why Poland could have had an allure for the Romanovs. Enjoying its first taste of independence in generations, Poland was perhaps the one nation on the periphery of Bolshevik Russia whose Roman Catholic majority might be expected to show the greatest zeal in sparking an anti-Communist revolution in the Land of the Czars — if there was ever going to be one.

PART IV

EPILOGUE

CHAPTER 18

LESSONS TO BE LEARNED

Any way you look at it, the secret rescue of the Romanovs was one of the nimblest sleights-of-hand ever pulled off at the expense of historians and the public. And their "assassination" was one of history's major subterfuges. In the wake of the years the whole episode stands as remarkable on a number of counts, including the diversity of nations that colloborated on it; the depth and duration of the secrecy maintained, and the size of the ample list of those who were duped.

There are many other "remarkables" of lesser consequence. Do any of them have a bearing on the realities of 1975, with our inflation and our energy crisis; our seething problems in the Middle East, and our persistent and awesome credibility gap between government and the governed?

Yes, I think they do. I believe there is much more of a connection than meets the eye.

But before grappling with the answer, let's concede in all fairness that the entire program of secrecy about the Romanov Case wasn't deplorable. Quite the contrary. There was an acute need for it in

1918–1919. Otherwise the once-imperial fugitives probably never would have gotten out of Russia alive. Likewise, the well-staged "execution," the mine shaft "grave," the official Bolsheviks "news" announcements about the decease of both parents and children — all were vital adjuncts of the same ruse.

Let's acknowledge that secrecy could have been a needed ingredient right on through the unsettled years of the Red-White war. Add another decade for good measure. That would give consideration to protecting the Romanovs from the "hit men" whom Stalin was so fond of deploying on distant missions all over the world.

By 1935, then, there was no longer any reason for the secrecy. By that time the chances for a royalist revival in Russia and an overthrow of the Communists by Romanov adherents could not have been taken very seriously by anyone inside the Kremlin. So from somewhere around the middle 1930s, the continued suppression of the truth about Ekaterinburg must be attributed to the influence of those who have a vested interest in keeping the facts bottled up for reasons other than national security. Their ability to do so far into the 1970s is one of the factors that give the case contemporary importance.

It's a fair bet that these same suppressive forces overwhelmed the Senate Internal Security Subcommittee when it issued subpoenas and was ready to dig into the Michal Goleniewski Case in 1964 and 1965, then cancelled its scheduled hearings when Goleniewski insisted on testifying about the Romanovs.

It's equally fair to assume that these same suppressive forces exerted themselves on the White House from 1971 through 1974 and brought one postponement after another in plans to release the Chivers documents.

In all the instances and agencies named, up through Watergate, crucial facts have been zealously withheld from the people for years.

Only the most strenuous efforts over long periods of time have gained a glimmering of the truths sought.

Officials involved in the concealment process have been more than willing for complete falsifications to become official versions of what happened. And some of those officials have imagined it was their bounden duty to lie about the issues, even when testifying under oath.

All this being the case, it requires singularly little genius to see what's wrong with the present situation in the realm of classified papers and clandestine operations:

Neither Congress nor the American people have the faintest idea what is being done around the world in the name of the United States. They have not fought for, or won, the legal right to find out what is going on now or what went on in the past.

The CIA is operating in flagrant violation of the law that created it — The National Security Act of 1947. There is not a paragraph in that act, or a sentence or a phrase, which authorizes any of the criminal activities to which the sprawling agency in Langley, Virginia has become so heavily addicted in recent years. The excuse that the President or the National Security Council or the Forty Committee ordered them to be done has no power to make them any less of a crime by our own legal standards, or those of the unfortunate countries on which they were inflicted.

The combination of all these circumstances has enabled a few persons in the executive branch to carry out manipulations on a global scale — often prodded by a few individuals with vested interests — which remain entirely unaccountable to Congress and the public.

The virtue of having a few professional agents like Riis and Koehler available for sensitive missions has been parlayed into a big circus of black operations whose failures are becoming notorious enough to make headlines every other week.

To see how to get out of the mess we are in, it is necessary to take brief note of how we got into it in the first place.

Richard Milhous Nixon was in the short pants of a five-year-old when the Romanovs disappeared from Ekaterinburg in 1918. It would be another five years before Henry A. Kissinger was to see the light of day in Germany. Nixon's troubles and the Romanovs' troubles, in the perspective of 1975, seem worlds apart, and at the time of the Romanovs' extreme agonies, they were, indeed. Even the White House was then occupied by a Democrat.

Yet the intervening years came to bring a curious link between the two sets of troubles. It is in that matter of government secrecy — how much is desirable for security purposes, how much comprises intolerable abuse of executive power, how much time must elapse after an event before we are allowed to know what happened.

Since the issues are due for debate in the next few years, it is well to be reminded that the Romanov Case is loaded with pertinent material. The case provides a living link between the era when American secret agents were a small cadre in Naval Intelligence, Army Intelligence (G-2), and men working for the State Department's Chief Special Agent — and, on the other hand, the era of the 1970s wherein the CIA is spending three quarters of a billion dollars or so annually on hundreds of sleuths all over the world, not only on intelligence-gathering, but on Mafia antics; the era of the 1970s wherein President Nixon announced (March 1972) that he intended to declassify a large portion of the twenty million government documents being kept secret (and didn't do any such thing); the later era of the 1970s wherein President Ford proclaimed that he was going to usher in a regime of openness and candor, and then a few weeks later (October 1974) vetoed a new Freedom of Information bill which would have given the public greater access to Federal papers.

You couldn't ask for more rousing assaults on government secrecy and excessive classification than those voiced by Nixon in 1972 and Ford in 1974. You couldn't ask for worse performances when their chances came to deliver the goods. These two leaders of the executive branch — both charmed pupils of Henry Kissinger — proved that we have arrived at an age in which Presidents believe it is adroit statesmanship to talk one way, and steer in another, wherever clandestine operations are concerned. They have veered to the Old World approach and its two cherished maxims:

"Secret operations are a game where anything goes and everything's denied. They're the one game where success depends on the myth of their non-existence."

These maxims derive from the practices of the Venetian princes. They may go back to the Stone Age tribes. At any rate, they were imported to Central Europe in the 16th century by the Florentine-born Catherine de Medici when she became Queen of France. The British embraced them after their own agents had been robbed, mauled and ambushed by Catherine's men in the back alleys of Paris. Adorned with a new cachet, and given a more fashionable life style with scientific overtones and university-bred operatives, the practices gained from the British a poker-faced smoothness which eventually inspired the phrase "perfidious Albion," a dubious compliment at best.

In two world wars the Americans tried to learn the game in a hurry from their friends in Whitehall. When they finally got the hang of it, they overlooked the most vital feature of the British approach — its invisibility.

To keep their secret intelligence services as unobtrusive as a sand crab at low tide, the British have used two weapons. One is the strict anonymity ceded to them by the government bureaucracy. The other is a law — the Official Secrets Act — which prevents all the public media from telling a story that the government wants embargoed.

For instance, you won't find the British Secret Service anywhere in the London phone book. If you were to ask a London bobby for directions to the Offices of the Secret Services' two main components MI-6 and MI-5 (roughly comparable to our CIA and FBI, respectively), he would give you a blank stare. The stare might not be due to the fact that he didn't know. It would be due to his shock at the thought that anyone would expect him to tell. Neither MI-6 nor MI-5 can be found under those names in any section of the national budget. The British Establishment keeps them just where it wants them — in the limbo of the unknown and unrecognized. To all intents and purposes they are fairy tales concocted by a few writers of spy stories — all fiction, of course.

The Official Secrets Act adds its legal weight to the drawn curtains. In this day and age the OSA is a screaming anachronism in any nation which claims to have a free press. It is one of those rules and rituals of empire-tending that go on and on, like the muscular thrashings of a dead snake, long after most of the empire has vanished. Passed in Queen Victoria's reign, and twice slightly amended, the OSA gives ruling politicians the right to embargo any stories "prejudicial to the security and interests of the state."

Few would want to quarrel with the "security" part of the law. Most nations have similar enactments, imposing heavy penalties on violators. But "interests?" That's the joker in the deck. It is one of the most flexible words in the language. It can be stretched to cover a herd of elephants, indeed, to cover the whole forested veldt in which elephants roam. Who decides what is "prejudicial" to those "interests?" The incumbent politicians in office decide. They would be less than human if they weren't inclined to view a journalistic exposure very embarrassing to them as one which is "prejudicial" to the "interests" of the state, and they have often done so.

There is no counterpart in British law to the First Amendment of the U.S. Constitution. Thus, in the crunches and clinches of controversial issues where a national scandal may be lurking, British editors can be very firmly inhibited by the Official Secrets Act and a formal notice from the Government (known as a "D-Notice") that such and such a story is banned. (Readers may recall that throughout the autumn of 1936 scarcely a line was printed in Britain about the romance of King Edward VIII and the American divorcée, Wally Simpson, while the American press covered it in great detail. Nevertheless the issue was vital enough to force the King's abdication.) More recently the paradox between British and American press freedoms became the frequent subject of a dialogue between newsmen from opposite sides of the Atlantic. Often it went like this:

British correspondent: "Under our form of government there never would have been a long-drawn-out debate over whether President Nixon should have been impeached or was guilty of a criminal act. Our Parliament, by a no-confidence vote, would have put him out of office months ago."

American correspondent: "Yes, quite true. But you forget that under your form of government Nixon wouldn't be in trouble. None of your newspapers would have printed anything like the Watergate revelations. They would have been stopped by the Official Secrets Act."

On this side of the Atlantic, where there is a tendency to overdo everything and spend too much on it, no such quiet self-efface-ment, no such genius for staying out of sight, pervaded our snoop-ing operations after we elevated them to the big time.

When the Americans finally decided to throw their hats into the international spy rings in 1947 (via the National Security Act), they did so with a bang. They installed the headquarters of the Cen-tral Intelligence Agency in a show place building in Langley, Vir-ginia which cost about $50 million. It's a popular gaping point on the bus circuit for Washington tourists. The CIA opened offices in all the big cities. It put its name in the phone books. It started re-cruiting on the campuses. Its alleged successes and failures are re-current issues in Congress and it's a dull week when stories about it don't appear somewhere. It has financed secret armies, airlines, shipping companies, political parties, educators, foreign corre-spondents, publishing enterprises, unions and as many phony cover firms as there are duck blinds on Chesapeake Bay. Without doubt it has committed far more serious sins than offering to help the White House cover-up of Watergate. But the additional publicity thereby engendered, the snake nests thereby revealed, and the backlash of indignation resulting, suggest that in its present form the CIA may prove not only to have been one of the most expensive agencies in the history of the U.S. Government, but one of the most short-lived. The tons of secret documents about its adventures will be jealously sought to be kept secret by the executive branch, espe-cially by Republican Presidents, if there are any more, until A.D. 2500.

It is almost unfair to the British to note that the CIA is an un-gainly weed that sprang from British seed; a wild, woolly and swashbuckling student reared under British tutelage. It is less un-fair to the British to note that most of its troubles derive from a gross violation of the British Secret Service's rule to remain always invisible.

Pending more drastic fumigations which are sure to come, each of the two longtime friendly powers has something to offer the other. The British should replace their Official Secrets Act with something like our First Amendment. The CIA should take a strong dose of the medicine which seems to make every agent of MI-6 and MI-5 crave anonymity and a zero profile. Otherwise it is doomed as an intelligence-collecting institution.

And if Britain and the United States are to continue their claims to be open societies, both must accommodate themselves to the notion that their actions are ultimately accountable to the people. This is another point which the Romanov Case drives home. For the opposite of this doctrine — the theory that there are some things which "national security" must hide forever — provides much too ready a means for crooks to steal the nation's whole treasure, with nary a soul being alerted until too late.

Heaven knows how many British Watergates have flowed past Parliament and Fleet Street as silently as the Thames because the OSA prevented their exposure. And as far as that goes, heaven knows how many other Watergates stole quietly past Congress and the American press in recent years because a "national security" label was put on them by the executive branch. We are lucky to have seen in this generation how persistent reporters can bare the hypocrisies of a racketeering and perjurious White House staff when they and their editors are confident that they have the backing of the First Amendment.

It is nothing less than incongruous that the spirit in which remedies should be made in our situation was well described by President Nixon when he issued his ten-page executive order on the "classification and declassification" of national security information on March 8, 1972.

"The interests of the United States and its citizens are best served," he stated, "by making information regarding the affairs of the Government readily available to the public. This concept of an informed citizenry is reflected in the Freedom of Information Act and in the current public information policies of the executive branch."

After outlining his new orders to the Federal agencies, the President observed that "We have reversed the burden of proof. For the first time we are placing that burden — and even the threat of administrative sanction — upon those who wish to preserve the secrecy of documents rather than on those who wish to declassify them after a reasonable time."

In the festive mood of this occasion, a White House spokesman declared that the new executive order was inspired by the only possible answer to this question: "How can we tell where we're going if we don't know where we've been?"

It would be hard to improve on these sentiments. All they needed was to be carried out in practice. Their resounding eloquence and the ensuing pitiful failure of their execution suggest that the lessons to be drawn are threefold:

A full-dress inquiry into the Romanov Case and who halted the projected release of documents on it should be included in the inevitable upcoming investigation of the CIA — and how the CIA should be restructured. I recommend the Senate Internal Security Subcommittee for the Romanov Case inquiry. Its members really owe it to the country. The Subcommittee got touted off the case by outside pressures more than ten years ago.

A permanent committee drawn from the executive branch, Congress, the Judiciary and the Defense Department should be appointed to rule on all requests by Federal agencies to keep documents classified beyond fifteen years. After the committee has caught up on the backlog of cases, the time limit should be shaved to ten years.

The United States has an intelligence compact with Britain whose terms never have been made public. It should be reviewed by Congress with a view to determining the extent by which, in responding to Whitehall's requests for secrecy on this side of the Atlantic on issues embargoed in London by the OSA, we, by our collaboration, actually impose the power of the OSA on our own fifty states. The protection of the sensibilities of the British Royal Family, for one example, is hardly an abiding interest or a security feature of the lives of the citizens of Chicago, Anchorage or Oklahoma City. There is a reasonable chance that the case of the Romanovs — relatives of both Queen Elizabeth II and her Consort — was entangled in this compact. Other recent ones *have* been, including U.S. documents on the Lusitania Case, and Operation Keelhaul, the Anglo-American agreement to repatriate forcibly Russian nationals taken during the liberation of Europe in World War II.

Four centuries after her own death, the methods, morals and pervading secret iniquities of Catherine de Medici may recede from the summit of the government of at least one of the "advanced" nations if Americans turn their indignation into political pressure. But the United States will be rid of them only if the people and the Congress insist that the CIA confine itself to the intelligence-gathering tasks allotted it by the National Security Act of 1947.

Allen Dulles, once a CIA Director, was more apocalyptic than he realized when he stated before an audience at Yale in 1958:

"The National Security Act of 1947 . . . has given Intelligence a more influential position in our Government than Intelligence enjoys in any other Government in the world."

Mr. Dulles might well have added that, far and beyond what the CIA was "given" by Congress, it learned how to take more — so much more that apparently its underworld outlook captured the imagination of the White House staff and the Committee to Re-Elect the President. But it is doubtful that even Mr. Dulles could have dreamed that by 1975 the black operations of our intelligence community would have convinced the CIA that it had the right to commit crimes in fifteen or twenty countries abroad which, if committed by an individual at home, would have put him in jail for years, if not in the death house; would have alienated a whole generation of youngsters; would have converted the image of the traditionally humanitarian values of Main Street, U.S.A., into that of a dark and Mephistophelian counterculture whose toxic influence was spreading around the world from all our foreign embassies.

This could never have happened if the executive branch hadn't mesmerized itself into believing that there were lots of things it could keep secret forever.

APPENDIX

BIBLIOGRAPHY

Accoce, Pierre, and Pierre Quet, *A Man Called Lucy* (New York: Coward-McCann), 1966.

Ackerman, Carl W., *Trailing the Bolsheviki* (New York: Charles Scribner & Sons), 1919.

Alexander, Grand Duke of Russia, *Twilight of Royalty* (New York: Ray Long and Richard R. Smith), 1932.

_____*Once a Grand Duke* (New York: Cosmopolitan Book Corporation, Farrar and Rinehart), 1932.

_____*Always a Grand Duke* (Garden City, New York: Garden City Publishing Co.), 1933.

Alexandrov, Victor, *The End of the Romanovs* (Boston and Toronto: Little, Brown & Co.), 1967.

Almedingen, E. M., *An Unbroken Unity, A Memoir of Grand Duchess Serge of Russia* (London: The Bodley Head), 1964.

Anastasia, Grand Duchess of Russia [Anna Anderson], *I am Anastasia: The Autobiography of the Grand Duchess of Russia* (New York: Harcourt, Brace and Company), 1958.

Anastasia, Grand Duchess of Russia [Eugenia Smith], *Anastasia; the Autobiography of H.I.H. the Grand Duchess Anastasia Nicholaevna of Russia* (New York: Robert Speller and Sons), 1963.

Anonymous, *The Russian Diary of an Englishman, Petrograd, 1915–1917* (New York: R. M. McBride, and London, W. Heinemann), 1919.

Asprey, Robert, *The Panther's Feast* (New York: G. P. Putnam's Sons), 1959.

Auclères, Dominique, *Anastasie, qui êtes vous?* (Paris: Hachette), 1962.

Aughinbaugh, William E., *I Swear by Apollo* (New York: Farrar and Rinehart), 1938.

Bencke dorff, Count Paul, *Last Days at Tsarskoe Selo* (London: W. Heinemann), 1927.

Botkin, Gleb E., *The Real Romanovs* (New York: Fleming H. Revell Co.), 1931.

———*The Woman Who Rose Again* (New York and London: Fleming H. Revell Co.), 1937.

Bulygin, Captain Paul P. and Alexander F. Kerensky, "The Sorrowful Quest," in *The Murder of the Romanovs* (New York: McBride), 1935.

Buxhoeveden, Baroness Sophia, *Left Behind: Fourteen Months in Siberia During the Revolution* (New York and London: Longmans, Green), 1929. *The Life and Tragedy of Alexandra Feodorovna, Empress of Russia* (New York and London: Longmans, Green), 1928.

Bykov, Paul M., *Posledniye dni Romanovykh* [The Last Days of the Romanovs] (Sverdlovsk, U.S.S.R.: Uralkniga), 1926.

———*Les Derniers jours des Romanovs* (Paris: Payot), 1931.

———*The Last Days of Tsardom* (London: Martin Lawrence), 1934.

———*The Last Days of Tsar Nicholas* (New York: International Publishers), 1934.

Churchill, Sir Winston Leonard Spencer, *The World Crisis* (New York: Charles Scribner & Sons), 1923–31, six volumes.

Cowles, Virginia, 1913: *An End and a Beginning* (New York: Harper & Row), 1968.

Deacon, Richard, *A History Of The British Secret Service* (New York: Taplinger Publishing Co.), 1969.

———*A History Of The Russian Secret Service* (New York: Taplinger Publishing Co.), 1972.

Dehn, Lili, *The Real Tsaritsa* (London: Thornton Butterworth), 1922.

Dieterichs, General Michael C., *Ublistvo Tsarkoi sem'i i chlenov doma Romanovykh na Urae* [The Murder of the Imperial Family and Members of the House of Romanov in the Urals] (Vladivostok: Vladivostok Military Academy), 1922, two volumes.

Dulles, Allen, *The Craft of Intelligence* (New York: Harper & Row), 1963.

Fowler, W. B., *British-American Relations 1917–1918: The Role of Sir William Wiseman* (Princeton: Princeton University Press), 1969.

Francis, David R., *Russia from the American Embassy, April 1916–November 1918* (New York: Charles Scribner's Sons), 1931.

———Reports and personal papers in Missouri Historical Society, St. Louis, Missouri.

Frankland, Noble, *Imperial Tragedy: Nicholas II, Last of the Tsars* (New York: Coward-McCann), 1961.

Fülöp-Miller, René, *Rasputin, the Holy Devil* (New York: Garden City Publishing Co.), 1928.

Gilliard, Pierre, *Le tragique destin de Nicolas II et de sa famille* (Paris: Payot), 1921.

———*Tragicheskaya sud'ba Russkoi imperatorskoi familii* (New York and London: Revel), 1921.

———*Tragiona sudba Nikole II i njegov porodice* (trans. Nikola Andric) (Zagreb: Kr. Zemaljska Tiskara), 1921.

———*Thirteen Years at the Russian Court* (New York: Doran), 1921.

———*La Fausse Anastasie: histoire d'une prétendue grande-duchesse de russie* with Constantin I. Savitch (Paris: Payot), 1929.

Graves, Major General William S., *America's Siberian Adventure 1918–1920* (New York: Jonathan Cape and Harrison Smith), 1931.
Grumbach, Salomon, Brest-Litovsk (Lausanne: Payot), 1918.

Hagedorn, Hermann *The Magnate — The Life and Times of Colonel William Boyce Thompson* (New York: Reynal & Hitchcock), 1935.
House, Edward Mandel, *The Intimate Papers of Colonel House* arranged as a narrative by Professor Charles Seymour (Boston: Houghton Mifflin Co.), 1928.

Janin, General Maurice, *Ma Mission en Sibérie* (Paris: Payot), 1933.

Katkov, George M., *The February Revolution* (New York: Harper & Row), 1967.
Kennan, George F., *Russia Leaves the War* (Princeton: Princeton University Press), 1956.
Kerensky, Alexander, *The Catastrophe* (New York: Appleton), 1927.
_____*The Crucifixion of Liberty* (New York: Day), 1934.
_____*Russia and History's Turning Point* (New York: Duell, Sloan and Pearce), 1965.
_____*The Murder of the Romanovs* (see Bulygin, Paul).
Kschessinska, Mathilde, *Dancing in St. Petersburg* (trans. Arnold Haskell) (New York: Doubleday), 1961.
_____*Souvenirs de la Kschessinska* (Paris: Librairie Plon), 1960.
Lasies, Joseph, *La tragédie sibérienne: le drame d'Ekaterinbourg; La fin de l'amiral Koltchak*, preface by Marcel Gounouilltou, letter preface by Général de Maud-huy (Paris: L'Edition Française Illustrée), 1920.
Lockhart, R. H. Bruce, *British Agent* (New York and London: Putnam), 1933.
Lockhart, Robin Bruce, *Ace of Spies* (New York: Stein & Day), 1968.
Luckett, Richard, *The White Generals* (New York: The Viking Press), 1971.

Majolier, Nathalie, *Step-daughter of Imperial Russia* (London: Stanley Paul and Co.) 1940.
Marie, Grand Duchess of Russia, *Education of a Princess* (New York: The Viking Press), 1931.
_____*A Princess in Exile* (New York: The Viking Press), 1932.
Markov, Serge V., *How We Tried to Save the Tsaritsa* (New York and London: Putnam), 1929.
Massie, Robert K., *Nicholas and Alexandra* (New York: Atheneum), 1967.
McGarry, William R., *From Berlin to Bagdad* (Portland, Oregon: International Publishers), 1912.
Mal'gunov, Serge P., *Sud'ba Imperatora Nikolaya II poslye otracheniya* [The Fate of the Emperor Nicholas II after Abdication] (Paris: La Renaissance), 1951.
Melnik, Tatiana, *Vospominaniya o Tsarskoi Semye i zya zhizni do i posle revolyutsii* [Memories of the Tsarist Family and Their Life Before and After the Revolution] (Belgrade: M. U. Stefanovich and Co.), 1921.
Moorehead, Alan, *The Russian Revolution* (New York: Harper & Brothers), 1958.
Morley, James, *The Japanese Thrust in Siberia* (New York: Columbia University Press), 1957.
Murray, Sir William George Eden, bart., *At Close Quarters* (London: J. Murray), 1946.

Narishkin-Kurakin, Elizabeth, *Under Three Tsars* (New York: Dutton), 1931.

Nicolson, Harold, *King George the Fifth* (London: Constable), 1952.

Obolensky, Serge, *One Man in His Time* (New York: McDowell Obolensky), 1958.

O'Conor, John F., *Nicholas A. Sokolov's Investigation of the Alleged Murder of the Russian Imperial Family,* including sections, translated by Mr. O'Conor, of *The Murder of the Imperial Family* by Judge Sokolov (New York: Robert Speller and Sons), 1970.

Page, Bruce, David Leitch, and Phillip Knightley, *The Philby Conspiracy* (New York: Doubleday and Company), 1968.

Parkes, Dr. Oscar, *British Battleships* (London: Seeley, Service and Co.), 1958.

Plowman, Stephanie, *Three Lives for the Czar* (London: The Bodley Head), 1969.

Preston, Sir Thomas H., *Before the Curtain* (London: Murray), 1950.

_____"Last Days of the Tsar," *Sunday Telegraph,* London, July 14, 1968.

Pridham, Vice-Admiral Sir Francis, *Close of a Dynasty,* with a foreword by Her Imperial Highness the Grand Duchess Xenia Alexandrovna of Russia (London: Allan Wingate), 1958.

Pu-yi, Emperor on Manchukuo, *From Emperor to Citizen, the Autobiography of Aisin- Groro Pu Yi* (trans. W. J. F. Jenner) (Peking: Foreign Language Press), 1964-65, two volumes.

Rathlef-Keilmann, Harriet von, *Anastasia, the Survivor of Ekaterinburg (trans.* Stewart Flint) (London and New York: G. P. Putnam's Sons), 1928.

Reilly, Sidney George, *Britain's Master Spy; Sidney Reilly's Narrative Written by Himself* (New York: Harper and Brothers), 1933.

Richards, Guy, *Imperial Agent: The Goleniewski-Romanov Case* (New York: Devin-Adair), 1966.

_____*The Hunt for the Czar* (New York: Doubleday), 1970.

Riis, Sergius M., *Yankee Komisar* (New York: Robert Speller & Sons), 1933.

Roberts, Kenneth, *I Wanted to Write* (New York: Doubleday), 1949.

Rodzianko, Michael V., *The Reign of Rasputin* (London: Philpot), 1927.

Sayers, Michael, and Albert F. Kahn, *The Great Conspiracy; The Secret War Against Soviet Russia* (Boston: Little, Brown & Co.), 1946.

Shannon, Margaret, *America's Secret Intervention in Russia,* article in the Atlanta (Ga.) Journal and Constitution Magazine, January 12, 1975.

Smythe, James P., *Rescuing the Czar, Two Authentic Diaries Arranged and Translated by James P. Smythe, A.M., Ph.D.* (San Francisco: California Printing Co.), 1920.

Sokolov, Nicholas A., *Enquête judiciaire sur l'assassinat de la famille impériale russe* (Paris Payot), 1924.

_____*Ublistvo tsarskoi sem'i* (Berlin: Slovo), 1925.

_____*Der Todesweg des Zaren — Dargestellt von den Untersuchungsrichter* (Berlin: Stollberg), 1925.

_____*So Begann der Bolschewismus, Leidensweg und Ermordung der Zarenfamilie* (Berlin: Deutsche Verlagegesellschaft), 1936.

Spiridovitch, Général Alexandre, *Les dernières années de la cour de Tsarkoie-Selo* (Paris: Payot), 1928, two volumes.

Strakhovsky, Leonid Ivan, *The Origins of American Intervention in North Russia (1918)* (Princeton: Princeton University Press), 1937.

Tarsaidze, Alexander G., *Czars and Presidents — The Story of a Forgotten Friendship* (New York: McDowell, Obolensky), 1958.

Tisdall, Evelyn Ernest F., *The Dowager Empress* (London: S. Paul), 1957.

_____*Marie Feodorovna, Empress of Russia* (New York: The John Day Co.), 1958.

Tokoi, Oskari, *Sisu: Even Through a Stone Wall* (intro. by John I. Kolehmainen) New York: Robert Speller and Sons), 1957.

Tupper, Harmon, *To the Great Ocean* (Boston: Little, Brown & Co.), 1965.

United States Senate, Internal Security Subcommittee, Part VIII, Hearings on State Department Security, containing testimony by two State Department officials on Michal Goleniewski's intelligence information (Washington, D.C.: United States Government Printing Office), 1966.

Viroubova, Anna, *Memories of the Russian Court* (New York and London: Macmillan and Co.), 1923.

Vorres, Ian, *The Last Grand Duchess: Her Imperial Highness Grand Duchess Olga Alexandrovna* (foreword by Her Imperial Highness Grand Duchess Olga Alexandrovna (New York: Charles Scribner's Sons), 1965.

Walsh, Dr. Edmund, S.J., *The Fall of the Russian Empire* (New York: Gordon Press), 1928.

Wheeler-Bennett, John W., *The Forgotten Peace: Brest-Litovsk, March, 1918* (New York: W. Morrow & Co.), 1939.

Wilson, Colin, *Rasputin and the Fall of the Romanovs* (New York: Farrar, Straus and Co.), 1964.

Wilton, Robert, *The Last Days of the Romanovs* (New York: George H. Doran Co.), 1920.

_____*Les derniers jours des Romanofs* (Paris: G. Cres et Compagnie), 1920.

_____*Posledniye dni Romanovykh* (Berlin), 1923.

_____*Russia's Agony* (New York: E. P. Dutton and Co.), 1919.

Wise, David, and Thomas B. Ross, *The Invisible Government* (New York: Random House), 1964.

Wrangel, General Baron Peter N., *Always with Honor* (foreword by Herbert Hoover) (New York: Robert Speller and Sons), 1957.

Youssoupoff, Prince Felix, *Rasputin* (New York: Dial), 1927.

_____*La fin de Raspoutine* (Paris: Librairie Plon), 1927.

_____*Avant l'exil, 1887–1919* (Paris: Librairie Plon), 1952.

_____*Lost Splendor* (trans. by Ann Green and Nicholas Katkoff) (New York: G. P. Putnam's Sons), 1954.

_____En exil (Paris: Librairie Plon), 1954.

INDEX

ABOUT THE AUTHOR

GUY RICHARDS has been a reporter and feature writer for the N.Y. *Daily News* and the N.Y. *Journal-American,* and at the time of his retirement was City Editor of the latter newspaper. He was educated at Yale where he wrote a column for the *Yale Daily News* and played tackle for three years on the Varsity football team. Following his graduation from Yale, he became a member of the Whitney South Sea Expedition of the American Museum of Natural History to the Solomon Islands and New Guinea. A few years later he was back in the same parts of the Pacific as a patrol officer in the Guadalcanal, Cape Gloucester and Talasea campaigns. He ended World War II as a Marine major, and is now a lieutenant colonel in the United States Marine Corps Reserve. Mr. Richards has written four books, as well as both fiction and nonfiction articles for many different magazines. He was twice honored with the Annual Page One Award for Outstanding Stories by the New York Newspaper Guild. The author started on the Romanov Case ten years ago, when writing a weekly column on international affairs, and "somehow," he says, "I've never been able to let go of it. I guess it was because I was never able to wrap it up. Mysteries can make addicts out of reporters as surely as drugs. All they have to do is flash a Mona Lisa smile — and stay out of reach."